Sunday, March 9th, 1862.

We sailed from Ship Island Friday night at five o'clock and arrived at this place yesterday morn about nine o'clock —

I have read and studied much of this river, but never did I think to see it; I am here now, bound for New Orleans at some time, when, I know not —

We found several war steamers here the "Hartford", "Brooklyn", "Miss", and others; we discharged two brass cannon on board one of the steamers which we brought for the "Itasca" and then took a pilot from the "Brooklyn" and steamed inside the bar about two miles and laid there all night —

In the night all the watch on deck were armed, the decks were cleared for action, sails unbent, spars sent down, guns loaded and everything made ready for a fight —

We knew not but during the night some battering ram might come down the river and attack us be-

YEOMAN
IN FARRAGUT'S
FLEET

YEOMAN IN FARRAGUT'S FLEET

The Civil War Diary of Josiah Parker Higgins

Edited and Annotated by
E. C. Herrmann
Guy Victor Publications

All rights reserved. No part of this book may be
used or reproduced without written permission
from the publisher except in the case of brief
quotations in scholarly articles or reviews.

COVER PHOTOS:

The Union Ironclad Galena
(courtesy of the Library of Congress)

Crew members of the Union ship Wissahickon
*(courtesy of the Massachusetts Commandery
Military Order of the Loyal Legion and the
US Army Military History Institute)*

Copyright © 1999 E. C. Herrmann

Guy Victor Publications
P. O. Box 22363, Carmel, California, 93922

Library of Congress Catalog
Card Number: 98-90801
ISBN: 0-9667063-0-7

Printed in the United States of America

FOR MY SONS, KENNETH AND STEVEN IBRAHIM

IN MEMORY OF YOUNG JOSIAH PARKER HIGGINS

With gratitude to Bill Breneman, for his support of my

desire and efforts to bring this private journal to public light

and to Martin Chester, for his photographic expertise

and to the staff of the Dudley Knox Library

of the Naval Postgraduate School in Monterey, California,

for their assistance with the research

to corroborate and elucidate Higgins' entries

A REQUEST TO THE READER

Should you have any information about Josiah Parker Higgins

or his family, the author would appreciate being contacted

through the publisher at P.O. Box 22363, Carmel,

California, 93922, or by email at eherr@redshift.com.

TABLE OF CONTENTS

Introduction 9

The Journal of Josiah Parker Higgins, January 1862 - July 1864 12

Postscript 79

Appendices

Appendix A --- *Chronological list of ships mentioned, unedited journal* 80

Appendix B --- *Chronological list of military personnel mentioned* 81

Appendix C --- *List of reading material received by mail* 81

Appendix D ---

    1A -- *Farragut's letter regarding Naval officer DeCamp and French captain* 81

    1B -- *Farragut's investigation of DeCamp's misconduct* 83

    1C -- *Confederate Wilkinson's recollection of visit with DeCamp* 83

    2A -- *Confederate Officer Higgins' report of mutiny in Ft. Jackson* 84

    2B -- *Confederate Brid. Gen. Duncan's report of surrender of Forts Jackson and St. Philip* 85

    2C -- *President Lincoln's letter to Congress honoring Farragut* 86

    3A -- *Naval officer Palmer's report of surrender of Baton Rouge* 86

    3B -- *Baton Rouge Mayor's response to Palmer's letter* 87

    3C -- *Farragut's letter to Baton Rouge Mayor* 87

    4A -- *Palmer's report of surrender of Natchez* 88

    4B -- *Natchez Mayor's response to Palmer* 89

5A -- *Porter's request for written policy on taking escaping slaves on shipboard* 89

5B -- *Navy officer's angry report of slaves on his ship forcibly returned to plantation owners* 90

6 -- *Farragut's explanation for delay of attack on Vicksburg* 91

7 -- *Farragut's reprimand of the Kennebec's commanding officer* 92

8 -- *Interview with plantation owner sympathetic to Union* 92

9 -- *Farragut's concern about scurvy's toll on fleet's crews* 95

10 -- *Report of the Kennebec's capture of the Albert* 95

11 -- *Report of ramifications of capture of rebel schooner pilot and the John Scott* 95

12 -- *Farragut's letter about difficulties preparing for attack on Mobile* 97

BIBLIOGRAPHY 98

ILLUSTRATIONS

February 1862 Naval enlistment information for Josiah Parker Higgins 42

U.S.S. Hartford, ready for battle 43

U.S.S. Hartford crew at quarters 43

Gun deck of the U.S.S. Hartford 44

Reconnaissance of Forts Jackson and St. Philip on the Mississippi River by gunboats from

    Farragut's fleet 44

Naval battle at Forts Jackson and St. Philip below New Orleans, April 1862 45

Waterfront of Baton Rouge 45

Canal Street, where Higgins strolled, taken from Royal Street 46

LCDR John H. Russell, Commander of the Kennebec until 1864 46

William P. McCann, Commander of the Kennebec in 1864 46

Captain Percival Drayton and Admiral David Farragut on board the Hartford 47

Death Certificate of Josiah Parker Higgins 47

INTRODUCTION

On February 8, 1862, the Kennebec was commissioned as a Union gunboat in the fleet of Rear Admiral David Farragut's West Gulf Blockading Squadron, a fleet of warships and mortar vessels destined to play a major role in the Civil War. On the same day, Josiah Parker Higgins of Massachusetts celebrated his twenty-first birthday by enlisting in the Union Navy and assuming the position of yeoman of the Kennebec. A month earlier, on January 7, he had promised himself to maintain a diary, to which he could confide his thoughts and feelings. ("…And a good Journal is a very rare thing, very rare indeed: however I only keep this for my own eyes so it does not matter so much…" – diary entry of May 7, 1862)

Thanks to his commitment, the following excerpted transcription of his journal is an eye-witness perspective of the Naval Civil War along the Gulf Coast. This evidently well-educated yeoman made few spelling, grammatical, or other errors and they remain unchanged in the transcription (examples: "McClennan", "St. Phillip", "predujice", "erassed", "bouy", and a stated weather temperature of "138"). The handwriting is uniform but often difficult to decipher due to the florid style and, on occasion, to the tossing of the ship in a sudden gale. Where a word or phrase is indecipherable or questionable, it has been placed between paranteses. Omitted entries are represented by a half-line of dots.

According to records from the National Archives in Washington D.C., Higgins and his parents were born in Maine. While probably in his early teens, Higgins and his family moved to Massachusetts, a move he lamented. He worked as a clerk in his father's store, but he pined for the snowy cold and dark evenings of his Maine childhood and criticized the worldliness of Boston. During his tour on board the Kennebec, he made frequent reference to people with whom he corresponded by mail. Among them was his sister Mary; he mourned the news of her terminal illness and the realization he would not see her again. He also referred often to a young woman named "Vine" with whom he had, to his regret, a rather uncertain relationship. Records from the National Archives indicate that upon his return from sea he married a "Lavina". Was this "Vine"? After her death in 1871, he remarried. A daughter, his only child, was born from this second marriage. Higgins was a merchant in his civilian life, living in Boston, Hyde Park, and Chelsea in Massachusetts; in Chicago; and in Dexter and Norway, Maine.

Higgins collected invalid pension as a result of "varicose veins of a severe type" acquired "…on or about the 15th day of September, 1862… in blockade service… aboard the U.S. gunboat Kennebec…" according to the signed pension papers in the custody of the National Archives. He died at age 54 in Massachusetts on May 13, 1895, when his daughter was eleven. The physician completing the death certificate wrote, "He had varicose veins said to be due to army life... Primary [cause of death]: don't know. [Duration of Sickness] some minutes." His widow, Florinda Higgins, collected a pension until her death in January, 1918.

As a young man living at home, Higgins had anguished for months over his inability to make a career decision and had weighed the prospects of going to sea. ("All I wish is to find a place where I can work to the best advantage, where I can strike and work hard—It may be on the seas —" – journal entry of January 11, 1862.) Although strongly advised otherwise by a close friend, he nevertheless went to the Boston shipyard, signed on with the Kennebec, and was at sea off the Atlantic Coast, past Pensacola, and at the mouth of the Mississippi within weeks.

Higgins immediately regretted his decision. Raised with firm religious beliefs and practices, he felt socially and spiritually isolated from his rowdier shipmates and starved for intellectual stimulation. ("I have seen enough of the U. S. Navy to know that it is not a fitting place for a young man: I have learned enough in reference to that to last me a lifetime. Such screaming; such vulgarity, such wickedness I have never heard or seen" – journal entry March 7, 1862). He longed for the peace and harmony of home. Welcome was the occasional newspaper or magazine he received by mail, such as the *Atlantic, Boston Traveler, Harper's, Time-Weekly Tribune*, and Bangor, Maine paper.

Resigned to the possibility of years at sea but hoping desperately for merely months, he expressed his frustrations and his experiences in his journal every two or three days for the next two and one half years. Clerking in his father's store trained him to be an accurate record-keeper; in spite of rough seas, seasickness, homesickness and despair, he conscientiously and meticulously maintained his journal. He itemized numbers of men wounded, masts broken, and bales of cotton seized. He noted frequency of coaling; Union ships encountered and Confederate ships captured as prizes; deserters and prisoners taken on board; deaths of officers and outcomes of battles elsewhere as he learned of them. Included is his brush with death not from enemy fire but from a large, displaced chunk of ice on the ship. Fourth of July celebrations are mentioned. He described with youthful horror the bombardment of the Confederate forts, and their retaliation, and conveyed the eager and fragile hope of all the sailors for mail from home. He commited to the privacy of his diary angry criticisms of his fleet's wartime strategy.

He also documented the friendships he developed with some of the men on shipboard; dawn's pastel light on the banks of the Mississippi River; the slate stillness of an evening sea. It appears that he inadvertently preserved between occasional pages of the journal small seeds of some kind, a tiny insect, and a sprig of leaves—well-dried and retaining a hint of green.

As yeoman of the Kennebec, Higgins participated in the attack on Forts Jackson and St. Philip, which guarded New Orleans. Following their defeat, he witnessed the lowering of the Confederate flag and the raising of the stars and stripes over Fort Jackson.

Farragut's victorious assault on the dual target dealt a crippling blow to the Confederacy. The fleet continued up the river to Vicksburg, participating in the bombardment of that city before returning to the Gulf and assuming blockade duty. Over the next year, the Kennebec captured several rebel ships or schooners that broke through the blockade, either bringing in supplies ("cigars from Havana") or exporting cotton.

There is remarkable corroboration of much of Higgins' documentation with sources available today. For example, he described the capture on December 9, 1863 of the Marshall J. Smith carrying 260 bales of cotton. The Dictionary of American Naval Fighting Ships, Vol. III, 1968, page 618, states that, "…[The Kennebec] shared in the capture of schooner Winona off Mobile 29 November and she took schooner Marshall J. Smith laden with 260 bales of cotton 9 December." Wartime correspondence between Farragut and other Navy personnel has been invaluable in explaining Higgins' entries. Most of the appendices depend on Charles Stewart's *Official Records of the Union and Confederate Navies in the War of the Rebellion*, published in 1904.

The last six months of Higgins' Navy duty with Farragut's fleet was spent at stations along the blockade of the South, mainly off Mobile. Having maintained a respected reputation until this time, he described a devastating conflict with a new officer for reasons he was not able to fathom. This most unfortunate turn of events exacerbated his desperation to get back home. His hope, he concluded, was futile. When he least expected it, however, he received discharge orders.

Higgins left the Kennebec for home on July 16, 1864 after a two and one-half year tour of duty. This edited diary transcription includes the initial entry from his return to civilian life; the actual diary continues for only several months but resumes in the early 1870's. Had Higgins remained on board the Kennebec for another three weeks, he would have been present at the attack on Mobile, Alabama, a notoriously bloody naval battle.

If that had been the case, Higgins' journal might well have been lost at sea. Instead, it was recently discovered in the basement of a California home, dormant in a dusty cardboard box beneath old photo albums, yellowed scrap paper, and sheaves of unopened 1940's gift-wrapping—an ironic sequel to his journal entry of January 11, 1862.

THE JOURNAL OF
JOSIAH PARKER HIGGINS

TUESDAY MORN, JAN 7, 1862
The commencement of a new Journal, and a new year. After thinking over the subject for some time, I have decided to begin a Diary this year, and I will endeavor that it be much better kept than any heretofore. I think it will be.

There are many reasons why it should be, among them, these. The book is much better than I have had before; this, though seemingly of small moment, is not so, it is of great consequence whether the pen glide smoothly over the paper, or whether it catch and mar the page.

A Journal should always be made of superior paper to ensure its being well kept. There is another reason why this should be a much better journal than the last. I am situated far differently. I could not keep (these) heretofore as I knew they should be situated as I then was and feeling as I then felt. It is over now—I trust forever—its memory is painful as it comes before me.

I wish in this, to keep a time record of my thoughts and feelings: I have never, as yet, done so fully in any Journal.

I wish to make it much more interesting to myself than the past: in short, I wish it to be my own private, confidential companion: my own secret communing with my own soul.

This then, is to be understood at the outset, O Journal: you are to start with me this year as a friend, knowing my thoughts, wishes, desires and cherished secrets—if I have any—doubtful enough, and yet it has been truly said—Every heart hath its own secret.

Come then let us talk with each other: we will be true to ourselves and to each other.

In my joys and sorrows, pleasures and troubles, hopes and disappointments, I shall come to you for relief. See that you give it me, for it will be too bad indeed if you and I are obliged to separate before your work is done: may it be well done.

How do we stand now? Are we where we would be had we our choice? I fear me, no. Hear me, friend. Know that on the eight day of next month I shall be a man for myself, in age at least, I fear I should say at most, for I am far, very far from true manhood. It has been my wish for months when that day shall come, that it find me where I could see my way (up) to Independence, that it find me gone from the business I am now in, forever.

I have tried many times but have been disappointed in all, I have written of them in the past all that I wish to say, and more— Since I wrote them I have written a letter, agreeing to go to sea if the person to whom I wrote think it best. I have not heard from him. Somehow I do not seem to care whether I do or not—if the truth must be said—and I have promised to give you my thoughts—I do not wish to go to sea, but if it seems to be my duty I shall surely go.

There then, O Journal, am I to be found standing in the market-place and seeking my "niche" where I may ensconce myself and thereby find my chief end, according to the "Autocrat":

A better than he has sung –

No man is born into the world,
    whose work
Is not born with him: there is
    always work,
And tools to work withal, for those
    who will:
And blessed are the horny hands of toil:
The busy would shove angrily aside
The man who stands with arms
    akimbo set,
Until occasion tells him what to do:
And he who waits to have his task
    marked out
Shall die and leave his errand unfulfilled.

The field lies wide before us, where
    to reap
The easy harvest of a deathless
    name,
Though with no better sickles
    than our (....)

O Friend! I believe in that doctrine, although it condemns the (....) I am serving. The great world is rolling and I am watching for an opening corner when it comes I am gone from here—so there—May it soon come--

SAT. MORN JAN 11, 1862
Well, friend of mine, I have heard from Capt. Aaron Higgins, who says that the "Augusta Norwood"—his new ship— goes to London: That she sails one week from to-day, and that he expects me to go in her. I heard this yesterday noon, and I went over in the afternoon to see him but did not find him.

I saw the ship, which is loading at Central Wharf. She is not a clipper by any means, nor do I think she will be a fast sailor; rather slow. I wish that I could state here whether I shall go or not, but can not: the folks do not wish me to go, and say all they can against it. but it seems, to me, an opening not to be neglected: I have been wishing for one so long it seems hard and wrong even, to let one go.

I do not wish to go to sea, but Independence may be there much sooner than elsewhere: I do not mean by that word riches, but to be free from depending upon others, to be able to do as I desire unstinted by want of means.

I wrote to Sarah last eve. for her opinion upon the subject, but I suppose the case will be decided before I hear from her.

Father has gone over to see Aaron I expect, and I may not have to wait long before I shall know, at any rate, not longer than a week –

So then you see in a week I may be upon the stormy ocean battling for "The easy harvest of a deathless name"

I have been thinking of that passage of Lowell's for some time.

It seems to me not to be such an easy harvest after all: it is a harvest that must be toiled for long and patiently.

In most cases I think, it comes not until after death, and it does not matter to the individual then what the world may say.

All I wish is to find a place where I can work to the best advantage, where I can strike and work hard—It may be on the seas –

TUESDAY MORN. JAN 14, 1862
I suppose it is settled for the present that I shall not go to sea: last Saturday afternoon I went over to the Quincy House and saw Capt. Higgins, who told me that he had sold the ship, so there was an end of that. He said I could have a chance to go with Howard soon

if I wished but I hope to see some other, better opening before he sails; he is on his way from (Havre) to New York.

I wonder what will turn up next for me, or whether anything will before Howard arrives!

The Walnut Street Sunday School are (...), arranging, and about to replenish their library. I have been to work upon it two evenings until ten o'clock, one evening last week at the vestry, and last evening at the vestry, where we took the books and carried them to Mr. Green's and worked, as they hold meetings in the vestry this week.

The weather yesterday and to-day is cold; The ground is covered with ice, and the walking is very slippery–

THURSDAY, JAN. 16, 1862
I received a letter from Sarah yesterday morning in which she urges very strongly against my going to sea, saying it is the last business she wishes a friend of hers to engage in.

I answered it last evening telling her I should not go, for the present at least, and giving my reasons for ever thinking of the idea.

It is extremely bad walking as it rained all day and evening yesterday upon the snow and last night was quite cold so that the streets are very icy indeed.

I was at Mr. Green's at work upon the library last evening until after ten o'clock; get ahead slowly.

Nothing new respecting the war but the papers intimate that a bold strike will be made soon, and it is high time –

In January, 1862, the Confederates were defeated at Mill Springs, Kentucky, by Brig. Gen. George Thomas, enabling the Union in early February to launch a brief and successful attack on Fort Henry on the Tennessee River.

MONDAY, JAN 20, 1862
I went to Walnut Street Church all day yesterday, but did not go out in the evening. Mr. Mansfield preached from "For we reckon ourselves (...) indeed unto sin, but alive unto God, through our Lord Jesus Christ"—and from "Go ye out into the highway and (hedges) and compel them to come in".

Neither of the sermons—as are none of his—were brilliant, but very plain. I have no doubt that he is a very good man, and an exemplary Christian but he has but very little experience in human nature: if he had ever been in business a few years he would not take many things for granted as he now does.

Father preached for Mr. (Chopin) at North Russell Street all day.

The weather for a week past has been quite stormy, rain and snow alternately and it is snowing now. It is very good sleighing and very bad walking.

I received a note this morning from Sarah in which she says she is very glad to hear I have given up the idea of going to sea: I may go after all although I hope to see some better opening: The prospect, however is as dark as ever ahead but I intend to wait patiently, yet longer.

Times change, and opinions with it, and opportunities desired in days past I no longer wish for: I think some humble path will open to me by and by, in which I can walk humbly and strive to do my whole duty toward God and my fellow men.

And thou—O Journal Friend—may have it recorded on thy pages when that time shall come, or perhaps it will not come until thy record is full but I trust it will come soon.

Learn to labor and to wait.
Longfellow

WED. EVE. JAN 22
We have had singular weather for a week, first rain, then snow, then rain again, and again snow, one after the other, but no pleasant weather at all: it has been snowing to-day but it does not amount to much.

I went up to "Carter Farm" this afternoon to notify Mr. Whittmore of a meeting at Mr. Green's this eve. on the library of the committee; there was one appointed Monday eve. but no one came.

It was a tedious walk up there: The snow is quite deep, and the sidewalks have not been cleared since the last storm, and it stormed then; altogether it was the most tiresome walk I have taken for a long time: it reminded me forcibly of country scenes in days long gone by, days when I was much happier than I now am, and can you give the reason, Journal Friend!

How the snow did use to drift upon the roads and fields of Maine in those years afore!

But we heeded it not, for it was nothing unusual. It fell much earlier in the season and remained much longer than here, and it came more frequently: piling up around the doors and under windows, blocking the streets for days together.

Then was the days of keen enjoyment! Then was a happy time! Of coasting down the hillside: of sleighrides on the moonlight evenings: of going to and from school: of holidays: of keen enjoyment all.

Oh! the bliss of sleigh-riding on a pleasant, moonlit eve. with one you love! And while the runner glides so smoothly over the snow, the hearts keep time with the merry bells!

I was too young for such rides then, but not too young to remember and to enjoy such as I then took.

O those evening rides I have taken with Father, as he went into some remote neighborhood to preach! In school and dwelling-houses, when the farmers and their wives and children assembled to hear the words spoken that would "make them wise unto salvation". That time was years ago, and years at my age which are apt to cause us to forget such things, but I can never forget those scenes in early life.

I seem to see now a small gathering, filling two rooms in the old farmhouse, where parent and child have successively lived for many generations. It is a pleasant Winter's evening, and the snow reflects the moonlight like burnished silver. They are gathered there from miles around—for they think much less of miles there than here, friend—and around the house stands half a score of sleighs with the horses carefully covered from the cold.

Soon the clergyman arrives and having seen to his horses, or, entrusted it to the farmers' care, he enters the house. How still! How peaceful is everything around!

In a few moments he arises, takes from the table by his side a hymn-book and gives out a hymn. It is a familiar hymn, one that the followers of Christ have sung as they journied heavenwards for years and years afore; one after another fall in and soon they all are together singing a sweet song of Zion.

After they have finished singing comes solemnly—"Let us pray" and every head is bowed while the servant of God pleads with his Master. The prayer ended he gives out his text and begins his remarks. What stillness, what attention: It is a subject which concerns all and they all hear it for themselves.

As he goes on anon comes a response: as he speaks of the trials and struggles which the disciples must encounter here each heart responds in unison, for they know by living experience that they must work out their salvation and as he repeats the many promises the hearts send glad response to the life, and when he concluded, with a glimpse of the nobler life to come rapture seizes them all, and then he stops and gives leave to those who wish to speak.

One after another arises and tells over his or her trials and joys and they take courage and go on.

The meeting ended they separate, each goes to his house with a resolve to live better than heretofore.

Ah! little do the city preachers know of the great joy of laboring among such a people. There is but very little sympathy with pastor and people here, but there they all love him, all uphold him.

Compare such a congregation as assembles in a city church from Sabbath to Sabbath and one in a country town and see the (...) difference.

How much better, freer, can one talk to persons interested than to those who heed not, care not.

But still the preachers desire city life and in many respects it is much more desirable; there are far more advantages for themselves and their children and we must not condemn in others what we ourselves practice –

I will end this long sermon, dear Journal, with a line of that beautiful tune,

"O the memory of departed days"–

FRIDAY EVE. JAN 24
I feel like jotting down a few thoughts now, while Father has gone to supper, and I know not what first to write.

I went over to the City this forenoon and had some card photographs taken, and an ambrotype, which, with one of the photographs, I intend sending to East Greenwich.

I have tried for months to obtain a good opportunity in which I could have, one at least, taken but have not seen one before to-day.

The weather still continues unsettled: have had no real sunshine for a long time, comparitively.

My heart has been sad to-day, friend: sadder than it has been for some time, for quite a long time. Several reasons are there why it should be so, reasons which I will not state now.

One event grows more certain every hour —I must be out of this as soon as possible.

MONDAY P.M. JAN 27
Last Saturday was a very stormy day: it rained very hard and consequently the walking was very poor indeed, as difficult as I can remember of its being.

In shoveling the snow from the roof of the store I got wet through all my clothes and was obliged to go home and change them, and one could not walk in the streets without going over the top of (ribbon) in water..

It froze some in the night and the walking was better yesterday. I went to church all day, Mr. Mansfield preached in the afternoon from "Thou art weighed in the balances and found wanting"

I do not remember his forenoon text. I went to Sunday School—did not go out in the evening, but stayed at home and read Boswell's *Life of Sam Johnson*, truly a great work.

I shall refer to it again –

WED. A.M. JAN. 29
After given up all idea of trying to obtain a situation in the Navy, I have again set out in that undertaking, and I mean to finish the scheme this time until I either see a chance, or, see that there can be none at all.

I have but made a start and nothing more: yesterday forenoon I went to the Mayor's Office and had a talk with Mayor Fay. He gave me a letter of introduction to a man in the Navy Yard, one Chas. Field.

In the afternoon I went over to the City and into Holway's, and requested him to give me a certificate of good character etc. as he is a Justice of the Peace and Notary Public which he promised to do, and told me of another way in which I might work –

I thought to go over to the Yard this forenoon but it storms, and I wish to get all the recommendations I can etc. before I go.

I have made up my mind to do something about this: to work hard: if I make nothing good by it I will make no harm.

I had much rather obtain a clerkship on the land but I will try the Navy and try hard— I expect nothing, so if it should turn out thus I shall not be disappointed: per contrary, should I get a situation I shall be happily disappointed.

One thing is certain: nothing can be done without effort and I will work with energy to get out of this (detestful) business—So, friend, here goes for good or evil. I go hoping, but not expecting; trusting, but not believing; for I know where there is one vacancy there is myriads to seize upon it.

I have made another beginning; I trust it will not come to the same ending.

More anon.

FRIDAY MORN JAN 31
I am no further along on this last day of the month than on the first; and I say it with much sorrow. I have not as yet been over to the Navy Yard, as the weather was stormy Wednesday, and as Father went over to the City yesterday.

The plan proposed by Mr. Holway has proved to be of no value, and if this other one do the same I know not how to go to work.

Somehow all my plans are frustrated and I can but wonder why? and what is it that I shall do in the future days?

Capt. Aaron Higgins was over here Wednesday; said the "Southern Chief" was on the passage to Boston from New York and asked if I was ready to go in her when she sails from there for London?

I told him, or rather Father did, how much opposition I met at home against going. He hinted to me that I would be sorry twenty years from now did I not go.

Perhaps I may: perhaps not. I would not be the man he is for all his wealth doubled ten times over. Nor do I desire to become obligated to such a man: far from it, nor will I if I can help it.

Well—I can stand it a little longer to see my expectations fade into thin air, but I hope I shall not be compelled to do this a great while. Every day but increases the desire; every hour but enlarges the hope; every moment but makes firmer the resolve to seize the first opening and to use it with energy.

This lying still, O how tedious! how dispiriting! how vexing to the mind!

O that an opening might come and speedily, in which I may act well my part in the great work(shop) of mind!

Come, and come speedily!

I heard a beautiful lecture last evening before the C-L-A on "National Honor" by S.W. Curtis of New York. Sent photograph to him this A.M.

TUES EVE FEB 4
I have a very severe head-ache this evening, but a much more severe heart-ache: both arising from a cause I never thought would come to me.

I have been over to the Navy Yard twice since I made an entry upon these pages: I went yesterday forenoon, saw Paymaster Bradford who said he thought there was a chance for me to go as "Yeoman" on the gunboat "Kennebec": I waited to see the Capt.

but he did not appear.

I went over again this forenoon but he had not been there this week. I went on board the "Ohio" and saw Paymaster Burgess, who appeared far from a gentleman, in reference to studying with him for Paymaster's Ass't—I did not make out anything and came home again. Mr. Bradford told me to call tomorrow. I do not know whether I shall or not.

I think this plan will fade like all my others.

THURS - FEB. 6

I went over to the Navy Yard again yesterday forenoon, saw Mr. Bradford, and Capt. Russell, with whom the former thought I could obtain a situation but Capt. R said he had (...) engaged a young man.

I shall probably go again tomorrow and see if there is any better prospect. I hope soon to get away from here. I hardly care to where provided I can enter my oar and row.

Spring will soon be here; perchance an opening may come with it—I hope it will be soon, very soon.

Capt. Russell is the man who burnt the privateer "Judith" lying at Pensacola Navy Yard wharf, for which he was promoted to the command of the gunboat "Kennebec"–

I like his appearance much and wish I could go with him in some capacity.

God knows what is best –

Higgins is probably referring to the "Judah", a Confederate vessel burned by the Union at the Pensacola Navy Yard in September 1861.

ON BOARD U. S. GUN BOAT "KENNEBEC"

KEY WEST FEB. 27 1862

Never did I think to commence a page on this, or any Journal, with such a heading as the above, but here I am. After going back and forth to the Navy Yard for a week or more over Sat. Feb 8, the day on which I was 21–I rec' the appointment of "Yeoman" on board this vessel.

I know nothing of the duties required, nothing of my station, nothing of the (...) but being very desirous to obtain a situation of some sort I immediately accepted this.

Were I to have it offered me now, and I at home on no account would I accept of it—knowing from experience what it is. I am in it now and will do the best I can, trusting, hoping, praying that very soon the time will come when I can leave it. I received my appointment on the 8th (inst) at about 12 o'clock; at 1 o'clock I reported for duty, worked all the afternoon Sat., all day Sunday, Monday, Tuesday and we sailed Wed. eve. about 8 o'clock.

We had a long passage, two weeks, from Boston here, tho' weather was stormy a great part of the time.

I was seasick most of the time, seasick, homesick and heart-sick all the time—we were out of sight of land most of the passage. I do not like (...) very well, and wish myself at home, or on the land at work, every day –

We go from here to Ship Island it is supposed. I have not been ashore as yet but it looks very nice their indeed, fruits of various kinds, and the weather is very warm indeed.

I have not felt like writing in my Journal before—nor do I feel like it now.

I will write again soon.

The location of Ship Island near the mouth of the Mississippi River provided an ideal site for Farragut's fleet to prepare for the attack on the two forts guarding New Orleans.

SHIP ISLAND MARCH 6, 1862

We arrived here last night after an unpleasant passage from Key West. We left there last Saturday noon. Saturday and Sunday the weather was very pleasant but it breezed up on Monday and the rest of the passage was very rough.

I was very sea sick Monday and the ship rolled more on Monday night than ever before; I shall be very, very glad when the good day comes round on which I shall leave her forever—May it soon come.

This is not at all such a looking place as I expected to see, everything looks hard; on shore it looks as though the soldiers must suffer. Nothing can be seen there but tents and sand and there are but a very few vessels here.

We leave tomorrow, for where no one knows, but I think to the mouth of the Miss. or thereabouts. We shall very soon find out—I wrote home from Key West and from here to-day and sent the last by the steamer "Rhode Island" which has just sailed.

SHIP ISLAND, MARCH 7 1862

I am very glad that I did decide to keep a Journal for it is all the confidential friend I have here. So far away from home, all the means I have of expressing my private thoughts.

I hope before I finish these pages, before the last page is reached that I shall have left the "Kennebec" forever. I have seen enough of the U. S. Navy to know that it is not a fitting place for a young man: I have learned enough in reference to that to last me a lifetime. Such screaming; such vulgarity, such wickedness I have never heard or seen: I trust that the high example I have had set before me for the past twenty-one years will follow me now that I am absent from them, now that I am away from home.

Home! Home! Home!

Never was there so much magic in a word as that to me now.

I think of it by day, I dream of it by night, it is always in my thoughts. It comes hard the first time absent from it, absent for no one knows how long. I hope to hear from them before we sail from here, but fear I shall not, I have not heard since leaving there, one month ago next Wednesday.

The weather here is very cold for what we have been having, almost as cold as it was in Boston when we left: it will soon be warm enough and much warmer than we shall wish to have it.

I suppose we leave here to-day: Each one has his own opinion as to our destination. Some may be right, some must be wrong, the probability seems to indicate for somewhere near the mouth of the Mississippi or Mobile Bay.

Wherever it may be I trust we shall do our whole duty, and do it well; that our friends at home will hear good tidings from us absent from them; that the "Kennebec" will live in story long after her bones have rotted back to dust –

"Success is a duty"--
"Freedom calls
    Quick be ready"--

MOUTH OF THE MISSISSIPPI RIVER, SUNDAY, MARCH 9TH, 1862

We sailed from Ship Island on Friday night at five o'clock and arrived at this place yesterday morning about nine o'clock.

I have read and studied much of this river, but never did I think to see it; I am here now, bound for New Orleans at some time, when I know not.

We found several war steamers here, the "Hartford", "Brooklyn", "Miss." and others; we discharged two brass cannons on board one of the steamers which we brought for the "Itasca" and then took a pilot from the "Brooklyn" and steamed inside the bar about two miles and laid there all night –

In the night all the watch on deck were armed, the deck cleared for action, sails (...), spars sent down, guns loaded and everything made ready for a fight. We know not but during the night some battering ram might come down the river and attack us but none came.

I remained on deck until eleven o'clock but there was nothing denoting anything wrong and I went below.

The steam sloop-of-war "Brooklyn" started to follow us in but ran aground and has not come over the bar yet.

This morning about ten o'clock the gun boat "Winona" came in and passed up by us and ordered us to follow.

We got under weigh and stood up the river behind her until we came to a small collection of houses called Pilot Town when both vessels stopped and a boat went from the other vessel ashore and brought off their men as prisoners. All this time all hands were at quarters and everything was ready for service.

We are now three o'clock—still going up the river. There is nothing but grass to be seen on the banks and we ascend slowly.

Launched from the Boston Navy Yard in 1858, the Hartford was sent to the Far East where she was a symbol of American sea power. At the outbreak of the Civil War, she returned to the United States to become Farragut's flagship. The ship was almost destroyed by flames from a fireraft which struck it during the attack on the two forts below New Orleans. Farragut and his crew were able to extinguish the fire even as they continued to bombard the forts.

MISSISSIPPI RIVER, MARCH 12, 1862

Last Sunday we went up to the head of the Pass and took five men prisoners and carried them down to the bar again. We laid there Sunday night and Monday we went up again with the "Winona" as far as we went the day before and landed the men taken Sunday.

When we went down again Monday night we anchored outside of the bar and laid all night.

Tuesday morning we went up again with the gun boat "Kineo" and when we arrived off the houses where we captured the men a boat was sent ashore and they informed us that a rebel gun boat came down the river Monday afternoon soon after us.

On account of the fog we could not see it; we anchored at the head of the Pass Tuesday night.

Just before night we saw the smoke of a steamer coming down; as soon as they saw us they turned about and went up the river again; it being late we did not chase it.

Everything was quiet during the night: about five o'clock the gunboat "Winona" came up and anchored with us. This morning about nine o'clock a steamer was seen coming down the river again and immediately all three of the gun boats were after her. We chased her two hours until she got up near Fort Jackson when she stopped, and our lookout could see seven vessels in sight from the masthead, and we could see another steamer on deck bearing down on us. Not knowing how many batteries there were, nor how much force we concluded not to go further, so sending a boat ashore to cut the telegraph wire upon its return we steamed down the river.

We fired two shots at the steamer while chasing her from the rifle on the forecastle, but neither of them hit her so far as we know she being so far off.

We took our first (Laient.) on board Monday night, named Blake; a young man and a good officer I hope.

SOUTH WEST PASS: MISSISSIPPI RIVER, MARCH 15 1862

On Wednesday afternoon we came down the South West Pass and anchored beside the "Hartford" and "Brooklyn" which had come round from Pass a L'Outre. We laid there until Thurs. afternoon when we weighed anchor and came up opposite Pilot Town, where we are laying now.

We sent a boat ashore Thursday night which found but four men in the place the rest having left for New Orleans.

Friday we took in coal from a schooner along side, and Friday night there was quite a severe thundershower. Today the "Hartford" and "Brooklyn" came up the Pass, or (...ither), went up from here and left us alone.

OFF PILOT TOWN, SOUTH WEST PASS, MISSISSIPPI RIVER, MAR. 19 1862

We laid here all day Sunday and on Monday went up to the head of the Pass. We found there the "Hartford", "Brooklyn", "Winona", and another gun boat came up while we were there, or, just as we started to return, which was about five o'clock. We brought down about a dozen Marines to Pilot Town for a guard over the spars etc. left there.

Yesterday, Tuesday, we went up again, and arrived at the head about noon; we laid there until about three o'clock and then returned.

The Commodore has gone to Ship Island; we can do nothing until he returns which we hope will be very soon; all hands are wishing to commence to do as soon as possible that we may get through and home as soon as circumstances will allow.

I had a real spell of home-sickness this morning occassioned by washing clothes for the first time in my life. Not only that, I have not heard from home since I came away and I never was so long before without hearing.

HEAD OF THE PASSES, MISSISSIPPI RIVER, MAR. 21 1862

It is a beautiful day, cool and pleasant, a real, home like day.

We were called this morning at five o'clock to scrub hammocks, and cold work it was: they are now dry and stowed away.

We came up the South West Pass yesterday and here last evening. Quite a large fleet of vessels came up the river night before last and yesterday: gun boats and mortar vessels: they went down the South West Pass and anchored off Pilot Town where we left them yesterday morning.

We saw a bright light like a fire up the river last evening. The Rebel Steamer "Star", which we chased, came down as far as the point about five miles ahead this morning and after looking around went back.

SUNDAY, MARCH 22 1862

We lay at the same place where we laid when I wrote before and there is nothing new: we expect to go up the river soon, how soon we do not know but we trust it will be before a great while.

The weather is quite cool, very cool for the time and place, almost as cold as when we left home.

I have been hoping to hear from home every day for some time but have not heard yet, trust I shall this coming week.

I long to hear, to know how they are and how they do, to know that they are well.

Friends seem dearer than ever now that they are away, and home seems far more precious now that I am absent from it.

May the war soon come to an end, righteousness prevail, and we return to home and friends. But may we do our duty, to our God and Country.

MOUTH SOUTH WEST PASS, MISSISSIPPI RIVER, MARCH 30 1862
Since last Sunday when my last entry was made, we have lain up at the head of the Passes: we came down yesterday to bring the Commodore.

We found twenty-five vessels of different descriptions, lying off Pilot Town, most of them mortar vessels.

Nothing unusual transpired while we lay there, excepting Thursday when we went up as far as we went when we chased the rebel steamer, accompanied by the gun-boat "Wissahickon". The Captain of the other gun-boat being longer in the service than ours he signalised for us to return when we reached there, we were obliged to comply.

We came down to the "Hartford" and reported to the Commodore and laid under the left bank as usual that night.

The next morning the Commodore signalised us to come down to the ship and we steamed there and took on board the Past Captain and his Clerk and went up the river again. This time we went up as far as possible, even within range of the forts, Jackson and St. Phillip.

Just before we reached the point, around which lay the forts, we sent a boat ashore to bring on board a man whom we could see from the ship.

He proved to be a Frenchman and after conversing a few minutes with the Captain he was landed again and we proceeded.

Soon after, or about that time we saw a rebel steamer ahead and fired a shot at her which fell short.

We then steamed up further and soon we saw the forts and they immediately commenced firing at us: they fired about thirty shots and shells; fortunately none of them striking us although some of them came very near.

We could see three steamers around a point protected by the forts and eight schooners anchored across the river holding a chain as we have heard.

After being within range about half an hour we came down again.

The Confederates had established a string of ships across the river, connected by chains, as a deterrent to the Union fleet.

HEAD OF THE PASSES, MISS. RIVER APRIL 4 1862
And so I date in another month, in April, month of showers.

Last Friday night we brought the Commodore up to the Flag-ship and Saturday the five gun-boats here, headed by the "Iroquois" went up within sight of the forts.

We laid there about three hours taking a full survey of the place and then returned home.

A French war-brig came up Pass a L'Outre last evening and is lying at anchor here now.

This forenoon the Commodore went down South West Pass in one of the gun-boats.

We are all anxious to know when we are to go up the river, but no one seems to know.

Yesterday I had a real home-sick day, the weather was fine but some how Sundays are days that make me think the most of home. I have not heard from them yet but I hope to hear every day.

SAME PLACE, APRIL 11 1862
Since I wrote here last we have been up the river and with five other gun-boats anchored all night within six miles of the forts.

The Captain of the French steamer came up in his boat while we laid there towed by the gun-boat "Winona" on his way to the forts to obtain permission of the rebel commanding officer to go to New Orleans to see the French Consul: we went up a short distance with him under a flag of truce but he wishing to go up alone in his boat we stopped and he went alone.

Soon after he was gone the "Winona" went up under a flag of truce but they fired at her from the forts and as they lowered a boat they fired at that.

The next morning the French man came down and said that they put him and his men in prison thinking them to be spies: he (tries) it again Saturday.

Farragut was mortified and angered at the misconduct of commanding officer DeCamp of the Winona, who violated Farragut's order by raising the flag of truce thereby jeopardizing both the French captain and Farragut's fleet. DeCamp at the same time had invited an old acquaintance onto the Winona for a visit who was, incredibly, Executive Officer Wilkinson of the Confederate ironclad Louisiana, which was sitting near the forts in readiness to respond to Farragut's anticipated attack (see Appendix D-1A). Farragut assembled a court of enquiry to investigate DeCamp's behavior (see Appendix D-1B). Wilkinson gave his own account of the strange visit in his narrative published after the war (see Appendix D-1C).

Yesterday morning we went down Pass a L'Outre and coaled outside the bar all day and all night and from the ship "Nightengale" a former (...)

Returned this morning.

MONDAY, APRIL 14, 1862, 6 MILES BELOW FORTS JACKSON AND ST. PHILLIP
We laid at the head of the Passes until Sat. morning when we towed a schooner a short way up the river and dropping her we came up and anchored off the ("Yusuf") where we laid until yesterday morning.

Altogether there were ten vessels—gun-boats most of them: yesterday morning early we got under way and came up guarding a surveying boat which was appointing a place for the mortar-boats to shell the forts.

While we were doing this the Commodore came up in the "Harriet Lane" and signalised us to follow her up the river: we were then about five miles below the forts, where we now lay, and we all followed him to the end of the point.

While there we could see two rebel steamers come out as far as they dared and then run back, we—our boats—fired several shots at them and into the wood.

We laid off and on all day, running up to the point and back again. We had dinner at two o'clock and supper at half past five and about that time we came to an anchor here.

It did not seem much like the Sabbath, nor does it any time: the watch were called upon to paint the ship outside in the morning and we should have had church services I suppose had we not gone up.

This goes very far to predujice the men against religion having to work and go to church the same day, and it is very wrong. There is no need of it and it should not be done.

There is predujice enough now against true piety without having it grown and enlarge: the officers are the examples for the men and all the examples they have. They should set a good one, so that men seeing their good works might glorify their Father which is in Heaven.

TUESDAY AFTERNOON, APRIL 15 1862
We still remain at the same anchoring, although yesterday we were running around here all day, first up then down.

I have a home feeling to-day, and not knowing how else to do that I may feel better I come to my only friend on board, even unto thee O Journal!

If I live, I wonder how long it will be before I see my pleasant home! Will the months lengthen into years before that time shall come?

God only knoweth.

There are many causes conspiring to make me think of home, very, very many, the surroundings are so very different, so much unlike.

A man-of-war is a very poor place for a young man to be, the associations are very unpleasant.

Not only unpleasant but disagreeable, often times disgusting: are these the stuff of which heroes are made?

You know not whom to trust the one you to-day consider your friend may to-morrow be against you. There is nothing so discouraging to our faith in mankind, in humanity, as that, to see the friend we trusted go over to the enemy. Alas for those who daily realize this.

Another thing: the sailors are not the stuff of which friends are made—I mean in a general way; there are as (...) friends who "roam on the dark sea foam" as there are ashore but the generality of them are not capable of great thoughts, and noble deeds.

To say that I shall be glad when I leave the sea forever is saying what I feel in all its strength now I would do my part for my country. I hope to do it well, but should I live until peace comes once more I wish, I hope, I pray, O Father in Heaven grant it, that I may turn from it into the paths ashore.

But my Father in Heaven knoweth what is best for me: I am willing to stay if it be His will.

THURSDAY MORN., APRIL 17 1862
IN SIGHT OF THE FORTS
We have moved up so far as to be near the end of the point and in sight of the forts beyond.

On Tuesday night we anchored near the shore on the right as far up as to be within sight of the schooners across the river and yesterday morning early we went further up and anchored on the same shore.

We did not remain there more than an hour when we got under way again and went to the other shore and fired several guns for practice: we were going to fire at the forts to try the range when the Commander of the "Oneida" ordered us not to do so as he had given permission to an English Commodore to go up and return within three hours.

We waited until the time had expired—and just as it expired he came down—and then went up within sight of both forts and fired at them several times.

We do not know how near to them we came but they sent a shell very near to us, full as near as I care about seeing, it struck just astern.

We then backed down out of the range of their guns and anchored.

After supper—or about supper time—three mortar schooners went up on the other shore and fired several times which the forts returned but did no execution.

We were under way all night guarding the fleet—which is now nearly all here—and looking out for fire rafts: this morning about five o'clock one came down.

It was a scow loaded with tar and other combustibles, and it came down among the fleet, the "Winona", the "Mississippi" and we fired into it and boats from the other vessels towed it ashore.

Things seem to denote that we are soon to make the attack—God prosper and protect the Right.

MONDAY, APRIL 21ST, 1862
We commenced the bombardment of Forts Jackson and St. Phillip last Friday morning and are at it now, with what execution we do not know.

I wrote here last on Thursday. Thursday night the rebels sent down a fire raft which did no damage whatever.

Friday morning they sent two more down just after the mortar boats commenced the bombardment: but they drifted ashore and did no harm.

The mortar-boats kept up firing all day but discontinued it during the night, very foolishly.

Friday afternoon we went up with three or more other gun-boats and fired several times and were fired at: several times we came very near being struck, the shots fell around and over us but none of them injured the ship.

The "Oneida" and the "Iroquois" were under heavy fire a long time and stood it nobly.

The "Oneida" was struck twice and had five men wounded: one of the mortar-boats had one man killed by a shell from the forts.

Saturday we laid still all day but some of the gun boats were engaged: the firing was kept up all night from the mortars: one shell from the fort went through a mortar-boat and sunk her, killing one man and wounding several I believe.

Sunday morning a deserter from the rebels came down to the bank of the river and was taken on board the Flag Ship: he reported that five men were killed the first day in the fort and had we kept up the fire all night Fort Jackson would have had to been evacuated as it was on fire and they worked all night to extinguish the flames.

Sunday morning at nine o'clock the Flag Ship signalised us to go on guard ahead of the fleet and we went up on picket duty for twenty-four hours.

We laid just ahead of the mortar-boats: the rebels did not fire during the forenoon but in the afternoon they sent shot and shell all around us. Very fortunately they did not hit us but many times they came very near it: three times steamers came down to the point and we drove them back, running up and firing at them.

In the night they sent down a larger fire raft, larger than the others: it did no injury.

Early this morning another steamer came down to the point and we ran up and fired at her but the shell fell astern.

During the fire Sunday a shell struck the main-mast head of one of the mortars and cut a piece of a man's boot-leg out there, not injuring the flesh.

They kept on firing last night: this morning the rebels commenced on as again but their shots all went over. At nine o'clock we were relieved—the "Iroquois", "Winona" and "Kennebec" by the "Verona"—"Wissahickon".

The sloops-of-war have not gone into engagement yet: I do not know when we shall all engage.

TUESDAY, APRIL 22 1862
We remained at anchor all day and all night yesterday, after we came to anchor, and remain here now.

The vessels that relieved us were fired at all day from the forts, and they replied and the mortars kept up fire all day and night.

No one was killed yesterday so far as I know: the rebels sent shots around us after we came to anchor some of them coming very near.

A boat expedition went somewhere last evening, I have not heard where. Three gun-boats went up night before last and unshackled the chain across the river.

Last evening the Flag Ship fired a rocket and burnt red, blue and white lights which two of the sloops answered. I suppose it was for the boats to start.

It is a beautiful morning: the trees look beautifully and the birds are singing sweetly.

Farragut directed Commander H. H. Bell up river on the night of April 20 to destroy the chains connecting Confederate hulls all across the river so that the fleet could accomplish its mission, which was to "run the gauntlet" past the forts and take New Orleans. Enemy fire from the forts and the river's strong currents deterred Bell from being successful, in spite of Union retaliatory fire upon the enemy. In a second attempt, Captain Caldwell of the Itasca managed to sever the chains on the night of the 23rd, permitting the fleet's move upriver toward the forts in the dark of the early morning hours of April 24. – Stewart, Charles, Official Records of the Union and Confederate Navies in the War of the Rebellion, Series I— Volume 18, West Gulf Blockading Squadron from February 21 to July 14, 1862, pp. 134, 135, 140.

WED. APRIL 23 1862
The bombardment kept up all day and all night: we laid at anchor all the forenoon and in the afternoon we slipped the spars, went along side of the "Hartford" and had one mast taken out.

After that we sent our spars and rigging ashore and then came to anchor. All the captains held a consultation on board the Flag Ship in the afternoon, and we supposed that we were going to attack the forts last night.

I think that was the intention but some how it was changed, why I know not.

I think we shall soon go up.

The "Oneida" was struck again yesterday and one man had his arm taken off and was wounded in the thigh.

Five of the gun-boats have their masts taken out: it is believed that they are to 'run the guantlet': while the larger vessels are engaging to rush by, if possible, the forts.

We shall soon know.

According to June 1, 1862 correspondence from Lieutenant Wainwright on the Harriet Lane to Commander Porter, the reason for the delay was due to the absence of the carpenter's crew from two of the ships. The captains' insistence on waiting for them delayed the attack by 24 hours – Stewart, Charles, Official Records..., vol. 18, p. 144.

FRIDAY APRIL 25 1862
The reason why we did not attempt passing the forts Tuesday night was that a sunken vessel drifted afoul of the Flag Ship and caused the chain to run out very fast thereby wounding five men who were around the capstan.

We remained at anchor all day and Thursday morning about two o'clock the vessels got under way and into line: the sloops forming one division, the gun-boats two.

We were in the second division, I believe, headed by the "Iroquois" and the "Sciota", the latter first.

Soon as I came upon deck I saw the signal from the Flag Ship, two red lights, and about half past three or four o'clock we started.

Immediately the forts began firing and kept it up until seven o'clock. Never in my life did I see or hear such a scene: I have heard of naval engagements, I have often read of them, but never thought to see one.

All the vessels run the guantlet excepting three, ours, the "Winona" and the "Itasca".

It was dark when we started and we were to follow the "Iroquois" which was to show a red light over her stern: as we reached the schooners across the river we ran into one and then into a raft and the delay it made brought on daylight: we were right in the range of the enemy's fire and (...) it was no time then to go on so we were obliged to withdraw.

The "Itasca" was struck thirteen times and one shot went through her boilers disabling her and scalding one man, that was all the wounded.

The "Winona" had four men killed and three severely wounded so she was obliged to return.

The "Kennebec" bears the mark of one shot but thanks to a good providence no one was injured.

The crew felt very badly that we did not get by with the fleet: perhaps it was as well—God knows.

We should be thankful to Him that we escaped so well—He knows what is best—let us trust in Him.

The vessels engaged were the "Hartford", "Brooklyn", "Pensacola", "Richmond", and "Portsmouth", sloops: the frigate "Mississippi", and the "Oneida", "Iroquois" and "Veruna", which rate as sloops I suppose, with the gun-boats "Sciota", "Winona", "Kineo", "Wissahickon", "Kennebec", "Pinola", "Itasca", "Katahdin", and "Caingu".

The "Harriet Lane" also engaged for a time but she did not intend to pass the forts as she is in the division of mortar-schooners, which remained behind.

All around us the shots flew thick and fast: I can not see how we escaped except thro' God's good mercy.

The firing ceased about seven o'clock: we remained in our old anchorage all night: just before dark the mortar schooners got under way and proceeded down the river.

We are now steaming around below the point.

SUNDAY, APRIL 27, 1862

Friday night we anchored at the Head of the Passes where we laid until yesterday afternoon when we got under way and came up just below the point. The "Winona" came with us.

While we were there a floating battery drifted down from above the forts. It was full of water and but little of it was above water: our second cutter boarded it with a boat from the "Winona" and went all over it.

Just at dark we ran down the river to where we anchored the night before and anchored.

This morning we came up again with the "Harriet Lane", "Winona", "Oneida" and two ferry boats.

The "Oneida" went up with a flag of truce and sent a boat to meet one from the forts: she has just gone down to the "Harriet Lane" and we are laying still—just below the point.

WED. NEW ORLEANS, APRIL 30, 1862

Here we are at last, where we have been trying to get for months; how long we are to remain here, or whether we are to proceed further up the river, I see no means of knowing.

Last Sunday night we anchored at some distance below the point: early the next morning a boat went down from the forts, in which were two men, officers I suppose.

Soon after we got under way and followed the "Harriet Lane", and two ferry-boats, followed by the "Winona" and flying a flag of truce, we steamed up the river and anchored off the forts.

And the forts surrendered: on account of a mutiny among the rebel soldiers, as they say, they were obliged to give it up, and at three o'clock, Monday P.M., April 28, 1862, the rebel flag was hauled down, and at half past three the stars and stripes went up.

We took on board the officers and two companies of the men and brought them to the city that night: the officer in command was Brid. Gen. Duncan and the next in command was Col. Higgins.

The forts' commanding officers were stunned and disgraced by the mutiny of the men, many of whom were "foreign" elements without any stake in the outcome of the rebellion. The continued effort against the Union at that point became futile (see Appendices D-2A and D-2B, the official reports of the surrendering officers Duncan and Higgins, and Appendix D-2C, President Abraham Lincoln's congratulatory letter to the Congress honoring Farragut).

We arrived at the city about eight o'clock and soon after the rebels were sent ashore: on what terms I do not know.

We are lying at anchor now off the city: the fleet are mostly here.

The inhabitants are very rank secessionists and do not hesitate to make their feelings known whenever they obtain an opportunity.

It will be some time before it will be safe for a Northern man to go ashore, but Butler will soon land his troops here and put the city under martial law.

The back of Secession is broken: their most important places are in the possession of our troops: they cannot much longer contend against the Right: God hasten the coming of Peace.

(No 9) Gun Boat went home last night with dispatches—may we soon follow.

Maj. Gen. Butler and his troops took over the city of New Orleans and the two forts, leaving the mouth of the Mississippi open to the Union.

OFF PILOT TOWN S.W. PASS
MISSISSIPPI RIVER, SATURDAY MAY 3 1862
We left New Orleans Wednesday noon, and came here for coal and provisions; we arrived here that night, about 9 o'clock.

Thursday we took in coal, and Friday we went outside the bar and took in provisions: we came up again last eve.

We supposed when we left New Orleans that we should return as soon as possible but we were ordered to Ship Island when we got here on account of a rumor that the rebels had congregated there.

I was very sorry indeed to be ordered to that place, as I wished we might go up the river and when we were afterwards ordered up the river I was much rejoiced.

I trust we shall go up now: we are cleaning the boilers and expect to leave for New Orleans tonight.

I hope we shall.

The weather here is very warm indeed: as warm as June at home but the awnings keep it quite cool on deck.

250 MILES UP MISSISSIPPI RIVER
WED, MAY 7 1862
Saturday night we got under way for up the river but we got ashore at the head of the Pass and remained there until early Sunday morning.

We arrived at New Orleans Monday morning and remained there until noon when we started up further.

We reached Baton Rouge last night at dark, and kept right on until after 9 o'clock when we came to anchor near the gun-boat "Pinola" which came up before us.

Six vessels are ahead of us and we are trying to overtake them. It is beautiful sailing up the river and I hope we shall go up as far as possible.

At Baton Rouge we saw, for the first time, land higher than the water: below it was much lower. The land grows higher the further up we go.

U.S. Navy Commanding Officer Palmer, who accepted the surrender of Baton Rouge, was irritated by the "arrogant tone" of the city's mayor and inhabitants and therefore landed a force in the city (see Appendix D-3A). Mayor B. F. Bryan's reaction was one of indignation at Palmer's intimidation as well as obligation to protect the city's citizens (see Appendix D-3B). Farragut sent a respectful letter to the mayor while backing Palmer's action (see Appendix D-3C).

This Journal is far from what I would have it, but somehow it is a very difficult task to keep one as it should be kept.

And a good Journal is a very rare thing, very rare indeed: however I only keep this for my own eyes so it does not matter so much.

I wonder what the folks at home are doing now, and where they are. I would like to be there when they hear that New Orleans is in our hands: it will be a time of great rejoicing in the North, great indeed.

I hope we shall go home when our work here is done: I do not want to lay around doing nothing: I want to go home and work.

Mother has written—"I hope you will not think of going to sea as your life's work"—my life's work —I wonder what it will be?

I would like very much to know that now, unknown. I would like, I sincerely wish, that when I get home I shall see an opening somewhere which I can improve.

I hope I shall obtain some situation where I can earn enough to relieve Father from the troubles, cares, anxieties of the store.

I am willing to work hard early and late to accomplish that, and may our kind Father in Heaven grant me it.

The Future is all unknown but I hope, in that respect at best, that it will differ from the Past.

The Past! The Past!
Words of dark, sad meaning –
The Future!
God grant it may be bright –

30 MILES BELOW NATCHEZ, (MISS)
SUNDAY, MAY 11 1862

We are so far along: arrived here last evening—the "Oneida", "Sciota", "Winona", "Pinola", and "Kennebec". The engine of the "Pinola" has given out and she goes back down the river this morning.

We hauled along side of her before daylight and took coal from her, as did also the "Sciota".

We have reached hilly land, the first we have seen on the river and it is very pretty, much more pleasant than the low land we have passed.

I feel as though I should like to be at home this Sabbath morning, and somehow this feeling comes over me every Sunday.

I miss my Sundays at home very much. Everything here is so very different and I believe I shall never lose this feeling, never.

There's no place like home
No place like home –

NATCHEZ, TUES MORN
MAY 13, 1862

We arrived here last night, or yesterday afternoon at four o'clock. We found no fortifications here and so the place was taken peacefully and we came to anchor off the town.

It—the city—sets upon high bluff and but very little of it is in sight from the river, but I hear that it is a very pretty place.

There is a ferry-boat running across the river the "Rosalie": by it our commanding officer sent a demand to the Mayor to surrender the city: the man who carried it was severly beaten on shore and our men went on board the ferry-boat armed and went ashore to demand satisfaction but the Mayor met them at the (...) and promised to surrender the city to-day.

Despite the messenger being severely beaten on shore, commanding officer Palmer found the mayor and citizens of Natchez such an agreeable people that he did not insist on hoisting the stars and stripes within the city (see Appendix D-4A). However, Mayor Hunter, while acquiescing in surrender, chastised Palmer for his formalities which "are absurd in the face of ... realities" (see Appendix D-4B).

THURSDAY, MAY 15, 1862
We still remain here, and this morning we are coaling from the "Brooklyn". I suppose we shall go up the river after we get through.

I sent a letter home this morning and hope I shall hear some from there soon but I suppose I shall not until next month.

I believe my homesickness, or the wish to be at home, is on the increase for I have thought much more about it lately than usual.

No wonder, for I am obliged to mingle with such associates, such company, it ought to make any decent man blush to think of it.

Well—I will stand it as well as possible, hoping that I may soon change from it, either to return home, or, into a better situation.

God knows which is best for me.

50 MILES BELOW VICKSBURG
SAT. MAY 17 1862
What are we living for? and are we gaining it? Can we answer this question as it should be answered by us?

Are we living for our own gratification? to obtain our own ends? If so we shall be grievously mistaken, and the time will come in which we shall see our mistake: see it in all its enormity. God pity us then.

What are we living for? Who knows! Who can answer the question as it should be answered?

Have we an object in life? And is it good, a worthy one –

If we live to the glory of God we shall live to our own good. Having this for our object on earth we shall reap an everlasting reward in Heaven.

God grant it.

I like my situation less the more I see of it: I dislike the situation, I dislike the company with whom I have to associate more than all.

O that I had a true and faithful friend in whom I could confide! to whom I might communicate my feelings –

I have none but you O Journal and in you I must confide.

I hope you will be faithful for faithfulness is very scarce now, very scarce indeed.

This spring weather causes me to think more strongly than ever of home, sweet home!

I wish I was there.

It causes me, also, to think much of "departed days"—days that were passed in pleasantness but the thought of which now causes pain.

You know O Journal: for why.

VICKSBURG, MISSISSIPPI
WED. MAY 21, 1862
On Sunday morning last we arrived off this place and ran up within six miles of the forts or fortifications which are in the heart of the city.

To the demand sent to surrender the reply came that they would not, and Monday we went down to communicate with the Commanding Officer.

We reached the "Hartford" just at night Monday and early the next morning started up with the Commodore on board.

We reached here this forenoon and took on board the Captains of the "Oneida" and

"Itasca" and Brid. Gen. Williams and ran up near the city to reconnoiter. No guns were fired on either side.

This afternoon a flag of truce came down —what it referred to we do not, as yet, know.

ON THE WAY DOWN THE MISSISSIPPI
FRIDAY, MAY 23 1862

It is a rainy day and I am in my "Storeroom" writing by the light of a candle for it is very dark.

This is the first real rainy day we had had since we came away from home: there have been days of some rain but this is a regular old-fashioned rainy day.

I like such days at home once in a while but not too often: such days in the country seem pleasant, I think, when "the men folks" are in the house repairing the farm utensils and all the family are together.

And a rainy day always reminds me of such days spent in the Pine Tree State — pleasant days they were.

I will stop here and write to Mrs. Coney.

JUST BELOW VICKSBURG
SUNDAY, MAY 25, 1862

It is a very pleasant day indeed, and I should be very, very glad to be at home.

The weather for three or four days has been much cooler than usual, I suppose on account of the rain.

Friday we went to near Natchez where we found the "Hartford", "Brooklyn", and "Richmond", and they all came up with us: we arrived here about noon yesterday.

Last night, about six o'clock, we went up to reconnoiter the town with all the captains, past-captains and the Flag-Officer on board.

We laid about a mile and a half from the town more than an hour when we returned and anchored (...) the fleet just below the town.

After we came down a rebel gun-boat ran down a little way and fired, but the shot went but a little ways.

BATON ROUGE, LA.
MAY 30, 1862

We arrived here Wed. morn. early and came to anchor off the town. The Flag Ship with us: soon after a boat from the "Hartford" went towards the shore and just before it reached the levee a company of horsemen rode down and fired at them wounding nearly every man in the boat: there was one officer in the boat, the Chief Engineer, he was struck three times.

As soon as they fired they turned and drove away, immediately we fired into the city and the "Hartford" followed suit and the firing was continued for about fifteen minutes.

We have heard since that we killed and wounded 27 on shore.

Yesterday the "Hartford" went down to New Orleans and left the "Kineo" and us here for guard to the soldiers on shore.

The other gun-boats are up to Vicksburg.

OFF BATON ROUGE, LA.
MONDAY, JUNE 2, 1862

We have not lain at anchor so long since we came from Boston as we have here: in no place have we remained longer than two days until now.

Everything has been quiet and peaceful since we fired into the city: troops have been landed most every day since.

Yesterday was quite a celebrated day here: night before last the transport steamer "Mississippi" arrived here from New Orleans with troops and yesterday two of the river boats conveyed them on shore.

Each regiment had a band and as they passed up by us they played the national airs which sounded very pleasant indeed.

After reaching the shore they marched to the State House, opposite where we lay at anchor, and took up their quarters in it and hoisted over it the stars and stripes.

Last evening the band played in front of the State House and it sounded charmingly off here, especially "Home, Sweet Home".

The officers went on shore yesterday all of them: they say there is but very little to be seen.

I do not care much about going but do want to receive the letters from home which I believe are in New Orleans: let me have them and I care very little of seeing Baton Rouge.

Summer is here: there can be no manner of doubt about that, and I wonder if we are to remain in the river through it all.

I have believed that August would find me at home again (...) nothing happen. I have that impression now. I hope it will prove true.

TUESDAY, JUNE 3, 1862

I have written once more to Vine I thought our correspondence closed but a week ago I rec. a letter from (L..) stating that she was confident that Vine loved me "as well if not better than ever," but her feelings were much depressed and other causes made her think her love had changed.

And I thought my last letter must have given her increased sorrow so I wrote asking her forgiveness if it do so.

To say that I rejoiced to hear that Vine had not changed in her feeling as I thought would be needless –

I pray that we may be again united if it is God's will, and that the old love may be renewed with greater strength.

THURS. JUNE 5, 1862

This is dull work lying here doing nothing, very dull work but it is better than rolling around at sea in this "wheelbarrow".

We should be better contented did we receive a mail from home oftener but we have not had one for some time and we believe there is one at New Orleans and we can not see why it should be delayed there.

Well—I suppose we shall receive it before long, and I hope mine will have good news from home.

On shore everything remains as ever: the officers go there every day and ramble around but "the men" are not allowed.

SUNDAY, JUNE 8, 1862

It is Summer time now without doubt, and hot weather must be expected: we have had it hot, as hot as 138 in the sun on board and I do not know how much hotter, but it will soon be mid summer and here it must be hotter than we have had it yet.

Last night I was very, very homesick, more so than for a long time and I have been thinking of home all day to-day.

It has been a beautiful day, like a June day at home: a cool breeze has been on the water keeping the air much more comfortable than it has been for some time past.

I wish I could have heard from home today I felt so much of the old home feeling on my mind but have not as yet: hope I shall soon.

I dislike the ship's company more than ever and trust the time will soon come when I can leave them.

There is nothing new here. I sent a letter home yesterday and have sent several since I heard from there.

Yesterday, and the day before, we started early in the morning for a bend about five miles up the river where there is reported a rebel camp but our engine giving out we were obliged to return without doing anything.

We have not means of knowing how long we are to remain here as we have not heard from the Flag Officer since he went down.

I think there will be no more sea fighting of consequence but there will be hard, terrific fighting on land I believe.

Our forces concentrating and the enemy being driven together they will meet on Southern ground and fight hard but, I think, peace will soon, very soon come.

And God grant it may.

SATURDAY, JUNE 14, 1862
I have been home sick all the week, and at no time more than to-day. Everyday causes me to wish, and hope, and pray the more for the time to come that will release me from the Navy.

Every day causes me to feel more and more disgusted with the men with whom I am compelled to associate—they can not be called men, many of them, for there are no manly traits about them.

I hope and pray for the time to speedily come when the war will be done, peace be restored, and we go home.

I care not how quick that time come now: I think our fighting is over now and the rest of the war will be carried on on the land.

I hope soon to have the great pleasure of commencing these pages honorably discharged from the United States Navy— discharged for ever and for ever.

The first of the week the Flag Officer with the "Brooklyn", "Richmond", the gunboat "Pinola" and the Flag Ship came up here, and are here now excepting the "Brooklyn" which went up the river yesterday morning.

Everything is quiet on shore: the river boats run up and down from Red river frequently.

We expect to start for New Orleans to-morrow morning: we are now discharging coal to the "Richmond" and we shall have to coal and provision in the city.

It is reported here to-day that Gen. McClennan has taken Richmond a large number of prisoners and Beauregard and Jeff Davis with them.

I hope this is so –
I want the war to cease.
I want to leave this company.
I want to get into business on shore.

Higgins was mistaken about McClellan taking Richmond. McClellan was right outside Richmond, the capital of the Confederacy, but was forced back during the Seven Days' battle that started June 26. The Union was not able to take the city until April, 1865, when citizens fled Richmond in the face of Grant's breaking through Confederate lines.

But if the war closing now will serve to perpetuate slavery I say let it go on. I am willing to wait.

Escaping slaves seeking refuge were often taken on board Union ships to protect themselves from being reclaimed by Southern plantation owners. The Union referred to these slaves as "contrabands" (see Appendix D-5A). However, for some time there were no written policies regarding assisting the "contrabands", which risked the safety of some of the slaves (see Appendix D-5B).

NEW ORLEANS, JUNE 19
THURSDAY
We started from Baton Rouge last Sunday morning at five o'clock for this city and arrived here at three o'clock that afternoon.

We had a beautiful passage down, the Sun shone brightly and there was a beautiful breeze.

One of the army bands came down with us, and played several pretty tunes.

We passed one house where the ladies stood in front waving the stars and stripes and the engine was stopped and the band played the Star Spangled Banner. It was the prettiest sight I have seen for a long time.

We came here for coal, provisions and stores, also for repairs on one of the boilers. We shall probably remain here about a week and then return to Baton Rouge.

Two of our men were invalided home yesterday and had a beautiful day to start with: I must confess that I almost envied them going home.

I have been greatly dissatisfied lately, much more so than usual and long every day to be forever relieved from these associations.

The more I see of man-of-war life the less I like it: and did I not believe I should soon get clear from it I do not know how I should feel.

I pray that if it be the will of God the time may steadily come when I may once more become a citizen.

I fear that this Journal will be full of complaints but I have tried not to have it so but I must write as I feel –

It will be over some time.

FRIDAY, JUNE 20, 1862

The weather is very warm here, but before long it must become much warmer: I dread for that time to come for it is warm enough now.

Homesick, homesick still: it grows upon me: Every day, every day I feel more and more discouraged.

The men feel the same as I: last night two of them deserted the ship: how or where they went I do not know.

If it were not that they have considerable money due them I believe more of them would follow suit.

I pray that we may soon go home.

JUST BELOW VICKSBURG, MISS.
SAT. JUNE 28, 1862

We left New Orleans last Saturday, one week ago to-day for Baton Rouge, as we supposed, but Sunday evening when we reached there the Captain of the "Kineo" informed ours that the Commodore had ordered him to follow him to this place: we started from Baton Rouge Monday morning early and reached here Wednesday eve.

We not fired upon on the way up as most every vessel is but we were prepared.

Farragut believed the fleet could not be effective in taking Vicksburg until the Union army had a larger presence to support his effort. He intended in the meantime to weaken Vicksburg, planning to blockade it and "occasionally harass them with fire" until the Army's arrival (see Appendix D-6).

We found the pretty little town of Grand Gulf destroyed utterly: too bad, it was a pretty place: nothing but the chimnies were standing.

I thought our fighting done, but this morning we went at it again. Before two o'clock the fleet got under way, and forming into line steamed up about the rebel batteries.

There were the "Hartford" – "Brooklyn" – and "Richmond" – the "Iroquois" and "Oneida" – the "Sciota" – "Winona" – "Wissahickon" – "Kennebec" and "Katahdin" beside the steamers with the mortars. As soon as we started the mortars commenced playing and when our fleet arrived off the town the action began and it was continued until nearly seven o'clock.

All the fleet passed excepting the "Brooklyn" – "Kennebec" and "Katahdin", who were left to silence the batteries while the rest of the vessels left up the river.

Farragut reprimanded the commanding officers of the three ships for hanging behind the rest of the fleet rather than pass Vicksburg. He was incredulous that the Kennebec's Lt. Russell misinterpreted his orders (see Appendix D-7).

And this was the greatest task: the fleet passing left us to fight alone, and we did fight thus for a long time. The "Brooklyn" ahead, we in the middle, and the "Katahdin" astern.

About seven o'clock we dropped down and the fighting ceased.

It was a pretty scene, early in the morning, that fight: it looked like pictures in history I have seen.

I will write more of this another time.

WED., JULY 2, 1862

I do not know anything else to write about the last fight more than I have written: some how I do not feel like writing much about it.

Everything was quiet Saturday and Sunday forenoon, but soon after noon Sunday the enemy fired several guns and the mortars commenced bombarding again and kept it up all day.

Monday they did not fire from the shore batteries, but some rifle shots were fired from the woods into the mortar-boats in the afternoon and the mortars fired their broadside guns several times at the woods.

In the evening we got under way and fired the pivot gun three times then anchored lower down the river to protect the river-boats belonging to our troops.

Yesterday morning we conveyed the tow-boat "Anglo-American" down the river below Rodney and are now on the way back.

Every vessel passing Grand Gulf now is fired upon so a gun-boat has to accompany them, but we were not fired upon yesterday. My feeling of dissatisfaction increases every day and I fear will make me really sick: I never felt so badly before, hardly. I hope I never shall again.

I dislike the vessel: I detest the service: I despise the men and they are fit to be despised many if not most of them, for such a class of men I never mingled with before and hope I never will again.

It is not only me but all hands feel discontented --

God grant I may soon be cleared from it.

I sent a letter home yesterday: hope I shall receive some soon.

JUST BELOW VICKSBURG, MISS.
SUNDAY JULY 6, 1862

The Fourth of July has come and gone, and a very dull day it was to us, especially to me: for I thought all day long of the pleasant way in which I have spent the last Seven.

All the celebrating we saw was in National Salute from the "Brooklyn" at 12 o'clock.

In the night, or, just before night, I was very, very homesick—feel better now.

We started early this morning to go down the river but ran askew just below Warrenton and are there now.

A steamer came down from the fleet this forenoon to tow us off but the hauser parted and she went back for a better hauser.

I think we shall get off this P.M.

SUNDAY, JULY 13, 1862

It is a beautiful, Summer Sabbath morn. and all the morning I have been thinking of home, sweet home. It's a feeling that comes over me more on this day than any other and as I prepared for "Muster" I could not help long for the Sabbath quietness of Chelsea.

I long to get home more and more every (s....ling) day: and pray for the war to cease, will the time to speedily come when I shall leave the United States Navy.

Every day do I long, more and more for this—God hasten its coming—I believe he will.

Last Sunday night with the aid of two river steamers we got afloat once more: the next day we went down below Ellis' Cliffs and returned here Thursday noon.

We were not fired upon.

MOUTH OF RED RIVER
JULY 17, 1862
We came here from Vicksburg, last Monday, stopping Monday night at Natchez, arriving here the following afternoon.

We are to remain until the "Tennessee" comes up, provided she come within a week: we are then to return.

The "Katahdin" came with us, and we are laying off the plantation of a, So called, Union man.

Months earlier, a most cordial plantation owner of considerable wealth was interviewed by a Union naval officer on shore. The officer was in search of food to purchase for the crew. The plantation owner regretted he had no food to spare, and in fact, was having difficulty feeding and clothing his 1,000 slaves. He welcomed the opportunity to speak with the Lieutenant and express the sentiments of others like himself who, having no allegiance to the Confederacy but rather to the Union, were under the thumb of hungry Confederate armies and threatening marauding mobs (see Appendix D-8).

Everything here is quiet.
And the home feeling still remains.

SAT., JULY 19, 1862
We still remain here, but should start for up river this afternoon or tomorrow, as we were ordered to be back at Vicksburg, Tuesday.

From there we shall be ordered down again, I suppose, to lie here, or, some where near here.

I hope we shall be ordered home before many months, weeks, or—I should like best of all—days.

But I see not prospect of it from some time yet, but it may come sooner than we think.

It cannot come too soon to suit me—I long to get clear from this connection, these associations and to enter upon my life's work—what will it be?

It will - in this respect - be one of the happiest days of my life when I get my discharge from the United States Navy.

SUNDAY, JULY 27, 1862
Here we are, but here we have not been ever since I last wrote here.

Last Sunday afternoon we got under way, and Wednesday forenoon we arrived at Vicksburg.

We found all of our fleet below the city, having run the guantlet down while we were here.

Thursday afternoon all of the fleet got under way and started down, the Flag Officer having received order to leave the river.

The first night we anchored just below Vicksburg: the second night just below Ellis' Cliffs, and the next day we got some distance below here when we were ordered to go to the protection of a mortar vessel which was ashore.

Last night the "Harriet Lane", the "Cayuga" and the ("Neville") came up and the latter (...) the mortar off.

This morning we came here with the

"Lane" and "Cayuga". The rest of the fleet has gone down. While we were down here a rebel ram ran past both fleets and anchored under the battery and is there still.

When the fleet came past one of Foote's iron-clad boats came down and one of his rams: there are both down the river now.

By stopping here we should have to wait much longer for our mail: I have not heard from home since May 17.

It is a beautiful day, and as I look into the woods I wish myself at home in the country.

And the wish grows stronger every day.

I forgot to mention that we were fired upon at Grand Gulf going up and we silenced the batteries in quick time.

GOING DOWN THE RIVER
SUNDAY, AUGUST 3, 1862
We arrived at New Orleans Mon. eve. and I received two letters from home: one from Sarah: one from Maria: an "Atlantic" from (...) –and two papers from home.

I wrote two letters home and one to Dexter—I believe there is another mail there now but we are going to Pilot Town to take our spars so as to go to sea.

Last Thursday I went ashore. The first time for nearly six months, or since we left home.

The Hospital Steward and I wandered over the city and went out to Lake Pontchartrain. We returned on board at 7 o'clock.

We started from New Orleans this morning.

PILOT TOWN, SOUTH W. PASS
FRIDAY, AUG. 8, 1862
I think it close to the day that I should write here, if only a few words.

Two years ago to-day I went to Provincetown on the "Acorn": Six months ago to-day I became twenty-one years of age: the same day received my appointment as "Yeoman" of the "Kennebec" and the "Kennebec" on that day went into commission.

As I look back upon the past it seems a long six months, and I have not enjoyed myself during the time but very little. I wish now that the time may soon come when the "Kennebec" and I shall part company.

I stopped on the Cape until the 19th inst. and enjoyed myself much, very much indeed: I have hoped I might visit the good old town this Summer but see I shall not be able.

We have taken in our mast and are nearly ready for sea: I think we will go by Sunday.

I dread being sea-sick very much but can only hope I may soon get over it.

Farragut was concerned that scurvy was eroding the health of the fleet's crews. Never does Higgins mention throughout his journal any fruits as part of the menu at ship's meals (see Appendix D-9).

I have a letter ready to send home which I shall probably leave here for the first steamer going North.

We have there mail at New Orleans but there is no knowing when we shall get them.

So on this anniversary day, many from home, I pen these lines in remembrance. When it again comes around may I be a better man and better situated: either is easy of accomplishment.

The weather is very warm indeed.

PILOT TOWN, S.W. PASS
FRIDAY, AUG. 15, 1862
We sailed from here one week ago to-day along down the Texas coast as far as Brazos.

We were fired upon from there and had quite a spirited engagement for a few minutes.

We went but a short distance farther

down and then turned back and arrived here Wed. eve. We are now coaling and expect to sail for Pensacola tomorrow.

I hope we shall have as pleasant a passage as our last.

I was not sea-sick while we were gone—hope I shall not be this time.

I received no letters by the mail which came down on the Flag Ship yesterday.

ON BLOCKADE, MOBILE BAY
AUGUST 26, 1862
We arrived here one week ago last Sunday forenoon and have been on the blockade ever since.

Poor enough is this anchorage: the sea is rough and we roll heavily all day and night—I wish we were out of it.

We found here the "Susquehannah", "Prebble", "Kanawha", and "Bohio": the "Prebble" and "Bohio" have since left.

We are off Fort Morgan which is thirty miles from Mobile.

We get under way whenever we see a sail and (...).

I received two letters from home the eve of our arrival: one from Sarah, one from (...) —have answered back.

Rec. a Chelsea paper yesterday.

PENSACOLA, FLA.
MONDAY, SEPT. 1ST, 1862
We came here last Sat. morn and it has been raining ever since: I believe this is a rainy place.

It is a different looking place from what I expected: the Navy Yard is destroyed, the town of Warrenton burnt, and every thing ruined which the Rebels could.

The former Fort Pickens is opposite and Forts Barrancas and McRae opposite it: I wonder that the Rebels (eva...ed) the place is so strongly fortified.

We are here for repairs, but so much rain delays us.

Yester afternoon I received three letters dated June 19th.

One from Mary
" " Maria
" " Naomi and Mary W.

It is a stormy day: home like enough. I wish I could (...) to be there.

THURSDAY, SEPT. 4, 1862
We are still here, and have done nothing as yet towards repairing the vessel: expect to every day.

I have received five letters since I wrote:
One from Father June 8th
" " " July 15th
" " " August 13th
" " Maria June 8th
" " Mrs. Coney July 15th
" " Vine " 24th
and two papers from home, one from Sarah.

I have answered Mrs. Coney's, Naomi's and Father's, but know not when I shall have an opportunity to send them.

I have heard from Vine: the first letter for seven months and I was very happy to receive it indeed. She says she knows not why she wrote the letter of Feb. 2 but she has no "change" now in her love. Thank God for that.

I will answer her letter the first opportunity and trust our correspondence will be resumed. Seven months ago I thought it was past.

OFF MOBILE BAY
SEPT. 18, 1862
We came here from Pensacola last Saturday: it was a very pleasant day: Sunday was windy with some rain. Monday was very stormy and Tuesday more so. Yesterday quite pleasant again and to-day very much so.

Tuesday I was very sea-sick indeed for the first time since we came out from home: it was very rough and I was very sick. The day before we left Pensacola I mailed a letter home.

One to Vine
" " (...)
" " Emily

and they went per the steamer "Ocean Queen": I hope they will all reach their destination this week.

There are six vessels here on the blockade - the "Richmond" which is Flag-ship – the "Oneida" – the "Kanawha" – "Pinola" - "Cayuga" and us: we expect the rest of the fleet will not arrive for some time yet.

We have no idea when an attack will be made upon the forts here but we hope we are not to remain out here much longer: it is worse than being at sea.

And we hear from home but seldom here but when we do hear it comes like blessings.

I have been trusting that the war was soon to come to an end but I must confess it does not look much like the end as yet: it may be (nearer) than I think.

God grant it may be.

The time slips very slowly away but it is nearing eight months since we left home: I did not think to be gone so long when I came away.

But if Freedom is coming than the war is progressing though we may see it not.

"God moves in a mysterious way
His wonders to perform"

I think He is moving in this.

PENSACOLA, FLA. SUNDAY, SEPT. 28, 1862
We came here from sea this forenoon. Night before last a storm came up as we were on the blockade off Mobile which lasted until last evening.

It was the severest gale I have ever seen, and I do not wish to see another as bad: it thundered and lightened, blew and rained in torrents, but we held on until morning when we parted our chain and lost one starboard anchor and finding that we were fast drifting on shore we hoisted the forsail a short way up and stood out to sea.

About this time something broke in the machinery, and there we were at the mercy of the wind and waves. Fortunately, the injury was repaired so that the engine could run and this just saved us: we came very near being lost, very near indeed.

It still continues to blow and rain and then we found the ship was leaking badly and the water for the boiler was taken from the (run).

It blew harder and harder, and early in the forenoon the smoke stack went overboard taking the main topmast and carrying away the main and main topmast stays, and very near taking the first cutter.

We ran out to sea as well as we could with the engine until later yesterday afternoon when we stood for this place.

We look very much like a wreck and it will require some time to repair damages.

I wish we could go North and I could get forever clear from the Navy.

Perhaps I may soon—I hope so.

I was very sea sick yesterday and have not felt well for several weeks.

WEDNESDAY, OCT. 1, 1862
One of the "golden days of Autumn". But the sun is very hot here, as hot as in a midsummer day at home: there the days must be getting cooler, and the fruit ripe and falling. When I awoke this morning a feeling of homesickness came over me, and has not left me yet: I think it will not as long as I'm in the "Kennebec".

I hope this will not be long. We were all day yesterday hauling alongside the Navy Yard

Wharf, and shall be all day to day taking in the "Winona"'s smoke stack which we are to have.

We should have been sent (...) for repairs, but Farragut says we must go to sea again as soon as possible.

But I hope for the time to soon come when Rear Admiral Farragut's orders will have no more to do with me than the wind.

I sent letters last night by the "Tennessee" one home—No. 2—one to Mary—and one to Shackford.

I hope the mail-steamer will arrive before we leave as I trust to receive letters in her.

I have not heard from home later than August 18.

I have not felt well for several weeks and do not feel well to-day: it would take but a very little to use me up now.

OFF MOBILE BAY
TUESDAY, OCT. 6, 1862
We came here on Sunday leaving Pensacola at nine o'clock and arriving here about three o'clock.

We took the "Winona"'s smoke stack and we had a (...) – topmast so we are in better condition now than we have been for months.

I sent a letter home the day before we left—No 3—and sent for a box of clothing, and sent an allotment of (110)—per month to pay for the same—I hope I shall receive it safely.

The weather was very pleasant while we were at Pensacola and warm: I went in bathing several evenings while we were laying along side the wharf.

So far it has been beautiful since arriving here: I hope it will continue so for rough weather is very unpleasant and I am not in too good health.

The mail-steamer has not yet arrived here.

TUES. MORN., NOV. 11, 1862
We do not go to sea this morning as was intended I believe: we shall probably go tomorrow or next day.

I was ashore Sunday afternoon for three hours and a great time there was: three men were allowed to go from each mess and a great portion of them came back drunk. One was kept in irons in the Navy Yard all night, one was bayoneted by a marine and badly hurt, and I came back sorry for going.

I went around the town, into the burying grounds, and the batteries and got back to the vessel about 4 o'clock.

We have taken in our coal and the most of the provisions.

FRIDAY, NOVEMBER 28, 1862
Yesterday was Thanksgiving. the first I ever passed away from home and I hope I shall be out of the Navy before another one comes around. The day passed off like all other days on board and had we not seen it in the newspapers we should not have known it was Thanksgiving.

I hope the folks at home had a good time, but I do not expect many of them were together.

The weather is quite cool but pleasant, and I trust it will continue so as long as possible.

The latest date I have heard from home is October 20.

WEDNESDAY, DEC. 3, 1862
Rainy today and warm: not steady continual rain but drizzle: in showers: now rain: now shine.

The mail steamer now several days overdue has not yet arrived: we look for her and trust she will bring us a good mail from home.

What a luxury letters are from home! How we appreciate them: read, reread and read them again and again: How we think upon those whose hands have formed the pleasant lines: their forms come up before us and we commune with them in spirit although the bodies are thousands of miles apart.

But time nor spars can separate us from those whom we truly love: "distance lends enchantment to the view" and we love them better than when we were together.

And in the night watches old times come o'er us, and we live the Past again.

It is even so with me to-day—nearly ten months from home.

....

FRIDAY EVEN., DEC. 26, 1862
We intended to go to sea this forenoon, but after we had got already something gave out in the engine, and we were compelled to stop until tomorrow when we shall make another start.

We have coaled, taken in provisions, and caulked outside since we have been here and the vessel is in a very good condition now.

I have written several letters since we came in but have not received any: the mailboat has not yet arrived, why we do not know.

It is a rainy night, a real homesick night and I wish, O how much!—that I could be at home tonight. Nearly eleven months! How much longer before I can see the dear ones! I hope not (unfinished entry)

1863
PENSACOLA HARBOR
JAN. 30, 1863
FRIDAY EVE.
My poor journal has been sadly neglected of late. I have not opened it since we were here before.

We came in here this afternoon from the blockade to coal and take in provisions, when we shall return.

Since we left here the famous "Oreta" ran out from Mobile, and the "R. R. Cuyler" chased her, and we have not heard from either of the vessels since.

We fear the latter has been captured.

Another steamer in attempting to run the blockade a few evenings ago ran ashore near Fort Morgan but she was got off after two or three days hard work by the Rebels.

Otherwise there has been nothing new since we left here.

I have not heard from home for some time, December 16 being the latest date.

There is no regular mail now, and we have to trust luck to hear from home.

This place looks desolate: there are but a few vessels here and everything is Sunday like.

I will try and be more mindful of this silent friend of mine in the future, than I have been, but I find journal keeping dull work.

But I do not believe as Beecher says—"It is an invention of the devil"—I think, rightly kept, a journal is an excellent thing.

And so we start for 1863.

PENSACOLA BAY
TUES. EVE. FEB. 10, 1863
We still remain here having been detained by Commodore Smith, who has received intimation of an attack to be made upon the Navy Yard.

FEBRUARY 1862 Naval enlistment information for Josiah Parker Higgins. *(courtesy of the National Archives; photo courtesy of Martin Chester)*

U.S.S. Hartford, ready for battle.
(courtesy of U.S. Naval Historical Center – U.S.N.H.C.)

U.S.S. Hartford crew at quarters. See entry of June 27, 1862.
(courtesy of the Massachusetts Commandery Military Order of the Loyal Legion and the U.S. Army Military History Institute – M.C.M.O.L.L./U.S.A.M.H.I.)

Gun deck of the U.S.S. Hartford. See entry of January 9, 1864.
(courtesy of M.C.M.O.L.L./U.S.A.M.H.I.)

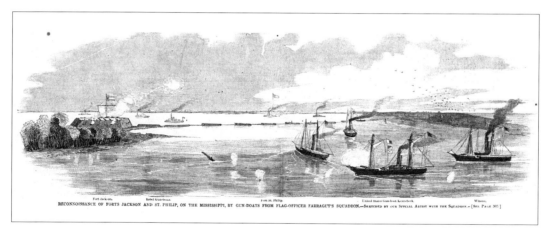
Reconnaissance of Forts Jackson and St. Philip on the Mississippi River by gunboats from Farragut's fleet. Kennebec is second from right, in foreground. Note Confederate hulls chained across river between forts. See entry of April 17, 1862. *(courtesy of U.S.N.H.C.)*

Naval battle at Forts Jackson and St. Philip below New Orleans, April 1862. See entries of April, 1862. *Drawn by (?) Parsons and engraved by Geo. E. (Perine), New York. Photo courtesy of William Breneman. From Headley, J.T., The Great Rebellion, vol.1, Hartford, Conn: The American Publishing Co., 1866, chapter 28, opposite page 368. Located in Dudley Knox Library, Naval Postgraduate School, Monterey, California. Source of original unknown.*

Waterfront of Baton Rouge. Note State Building at far right, occupied by the Union and across from which the Kennebec was anchored. See entry of June 2, 1862. *(courtesy of Andrew D. Lytle Collection, Louisiana and Lower Mississippi Valley Collections, L.S.U. Libraries, Louisiana State University, Baton Rouge, LA)*

46 YEOMAN IN FARRAGUT'S FLEET

Canal Street, where Higgins strolled, taken from Royal Street. Smokestacks of ships are visible at wharf end of street. See entry of August 28, 1863. *(courtesy of M.C.M.O.L.L./U.S.A.M.H.I.)*

LCDR John H. Russell, Commander of the Kennebec until 1864. Higgins signed on with Russell in Boston in 1862 and initially held him in high regard. See entry of February 6, 1862. *(courtesy of U.S.N.H.C.)*

William P. McCann, Commander of the Kennebec in 1864, with whom Higgins had a falling-out. See entry of November 8, 1863. *(courtesy of U.S.N.H.C.)*

Captain Percival Drayton and Admiral David Farragut on board the Hartford. Higgins intended to appeal to both Drayton and Farragut to assist him in separating from the Navy. Farragut responded to Higgins' request. See entries of May 14 and July 5, 1864. *(courtesy of M.C.M.O.L.L./U.S.A.M.H.I.)*

Death certificate of Josiah Parker Higgins, May 1895.
(courtesy of the National Archives; photo courtesy of Martin Chester)

We sail around the bay, up to Pensacola and back etc. etc. but have seen no signs of any of the enemy as yet.

My twenty second birth day has come and gone, and I feel older than before somehow. This is the second birthday I have spent in the Navy. I hope before another shall come, I shall be clear of the institution; a long time before.

It is much pleasanter here than off Mobile, and I hope we shall remain.

....

BLOCKADING MOBILE BAY.
WED. EVE. MARCH 4, 1863
The latter part of February was quite unpleasant, but so far this month the weather has been very pleasant, and the sea very smooth.

The "Union" returned to-day from the river, and by her I received a *Boston Traveller* of February 7th but no letters.

I hope to receive letters soon, but I see no way to receive them from New Orleans were there any there, as I hope there is.

There is nothing of much interest here: two or three schooners have run the blockade lately.

The "Lackawanna" arrived here to-day from Pensacola, and will relieve the "Susquehannah" I suppose. And it is also reported that the "Colerado" is on the way here.

I hope to hear soon that Charleston and Savannah are in our possession.

The Confederates defending Fort Sumter protected Charleston against Union attack, although the fort sustained significant damage. Charleston was finally evacuated in February 1865, its citizens forced out by Sherman's armies. Savannah fell to Sherman on his famed march to the sea, days before Christmas of 1864. Savannah was an important transportation center for the South; its waterways, roadways and railroads allowed access up and down the coast as well as inland.

(At this point, Higgins changes to lead rather than ink, and the script becomes smaller and less uniform.)

24TH
Was pleasant most of the day. In the early part of the forenoon a strange sail was reported coming from the Westward, and the "Colorado" signalised us to chase. It proved to be the steamer ("F...man") from New Orleans to Pensacola: from her we heard that Admiral Farragut had been past Port Hudson with two vessels: that the rest of the fleet failed to pass: and that the "Mississippi" ran ashore and was blown up by her Commander. During the first part of the night the wind blew very strong from the North West.

Port Hudson, a short distance from Baton Rouge, was an important site as it guarded the Mississippi River. Farragut bombarded it on his way upriver to Vicksburg.

However, the still, overcast night at Port Hudson prohibited dissipation of smoke from guns and cannon; the men on board the ships were unable to adequately visualize their targets, leading to confusion and misinformation. Consequently, the Union "Mississippi" was attacked by both friendly and enemy fire as it turned back and it eventually ran aground. After the transfer of men off the ship, it was set on fire. Subsequent bombardment again in May led to the surrender of Port Hudson in July 1863.

....

26TH
Quite pleasant did not get under way during the day.

(A small bug was preserved right under this entry.)

(APRIL) 14
This morning, between two and three o'clock a steamer ran in. She was first seen by the man at the mast-head who reported her.

All hands were called to quarters. The chain was slipped and we started in pursuit, firing as we went.

We chased her very near the fort, but it was very dark so that we could not see her after she ran ahead of us.

She got in, and we do not know whether she was struck by one shot or not. I have no doubt she could easily have been taken had it not been for the stupidity of the Captain, who swung the vessel in the wrong direction.

Soon after 3 o'clock we returned to our station, and anchored until about 6 o'clock when we ran further out and anchored: the wind blowing harder we hove up and ran out still further in the afternoon; soon after 8 o'clock we ran in again.

(MAY) 4
A very pleasant day.

We laid at one station until about 5 o'clock, P.M. When a sail was discovered at the Eastward: we signalised and gave chase, the "Kanawha" (being) at the Flag-ship and she proved to be the sch. "Sam Houston", and when we neared her we discovered another further out, and standing in shore.

We stood for her, and when we came near enough we fired: she did not alter her course and we fired several times.

At last she altered her course and stood for us, setting her (ga..-topsail) and staysail: but she kept heading for the shore, and we kept on firing.

A shell struck fast going into the Pivot Gun, disabling that for the time, but we kept firing from the Parrot until we came up to her and she (...) too.

We sent a boat on board and found she was the sch. "Jupiter" from Havana bound to Miss.

The first prize for the "Kennebec".

10
Very pleasant indeed: we got under way about 4 o'clock and anchored further from land, and ran in again after dark.

Had church services at muster in the forenoon.

MAY 11
Very pleasant: we got under way about 9 o'clock and went to the Flag-ship, where we anchored until afternoon, when we proceeded to the "Aroostook", and anchored, where we remained until 6 o'clock when we took our station.

We heard at the flag-ship via Rebel sources, that our troops had had another battle at Fredericksburg which they claim: that Van Dorn had been assaniated, and "Stonewall Jackson" lost an arm.

On May 2, "Stonewall" Jackson and some of his men were fired upon at nightime outside Chancellorsville by a Confederate regiment that mistook Jackson and his men for Union troops. Jackson died of his wounds on May 10. Major General Van Dorn was murdered while working at his desk at military headquarters by a civilian doctor; it was rumored that the fatal shot to his head was the result of his interest in the assassin's wife – Foote, Shelby, The Civil War, p. 178.

....

MAY 16
Quite pleasant: we got under way in the morning and anchored near the Flag-ship where we remained until nearly dark when we took our station.

17
Quite pleasant: we laid at anchor all day: had muster at church services at 10 o'clock.

18
This morning before daylight there was a vessel burning near Fort Morgan, which we learned was (bombed) by a boat from the "R.R. "Cuyler", the officers and men taken prisoners and the vessel burnt while she had (...) - out with which she was trying to (work) ashore.

I heard the officer in charge of the boat was a Master's Mate - but I am not certain of his name: it was a (...) as the vessel was very near the fort.

Soon after the "Aroostook" captured a small schooner running out with cotton also, and later in the day the "Kanawha" came in with another, which she had chased outside.

We took a lot of officers and men from the "Colorado" and carried them to (P..ing) Pass fishing: they got a large number in the (swim).

When we returned we found the sch. "Sam Houston" had came from New Orleans, but I was much disappointed in receiving no mail by her.

....

20
We got under way this morning at 4 o'clock and anchored farther from the land. We remained there until about 10 o'clock when a sail was discovered at the S.E. We got under way and went to her, finding she was the government sch. "Independence" from Pensacola we stood out to sea for another sail, which we discovered while chasing the first.

We got near enough to see it was a side wheel steamer burning coal making a black smoke but she ran away, and out of sight of us in a short time so that we abandoned the chase.

We continued to the Flag-ship, but did not anchor, and went to the "Aroostook" and anchored.

21
We lied at anchor all day: very rough—a flag of truce came out from Mobile.

....

25
We squared (retlims), and painted ship outside to-day: weather windy and cloudy.

The steamer "United - States", from New Orleans, came down the river early in the morning and went to sea: no steamers came in: several sailing vessels towed over the bar during the day.

In the afternoon we received an "Extra (E..)" from New Orleans informing us of Grant's taking two batteries at Vicksburg and (100) guns, and of an engagement near Port Hudson. All the signs are encouraging and I hope we shall hear before leaving the river that the whole river is (ours).

Farragut's fleet had gone up the Mississippi in May 1862 to attack Vicksburg. Although poorly defended, Vicksburg refused to surrender and Farragut sailed south. The Union continued the campaign against the city. Grant later tried twice to take Vicksburg, but was unsuccessful both times. Changing tactics, he decided to starve the city. Union troops surrounded Vicksburg on land and the Union Navy was in force on the river. After one of the longest sieges of the war, on July 4, 1863 Vicksburg surrendered unconditionally. With the surrender of Port Hudson on July 9, the Union controlled the entire Mississippi River and the Confederacy was split in half.

....

28

Pleasant: Mr. (T...) arrived in the morning by a tow from New Orleans, but the rest of the officers have not yet arrived.

They sent a dispatch to-day saying they would come down to-day. Last evening we had a telegram that our troops were fighting at Port Hudson: that they had been repulsed five times and are still fighting. It sprinkled in the evening.

....

JUNE 1

Warm and pleasant—we got under way before daylight and anchored further from shore, and ran in again after dark.

We heard in the evening of the death of Wm Brooks our Executive Officer for a short time, and Acting Master, who has been absent some time in a prize schooner to Key West.

His sudden death was a severe shock to all hands: he was a very popular man, officer on board, and his loss will be severely felt.

He died on board the "Magnolia" in Key West, Fla.

2

Pleasant and warm. We got under way in the morning and anchored further from land, and near the "Kanawha."

About 10 o'clock we went to the Flag-ship where we anchored until after dinner.

The chief Engineer came on board to see the difficulty with our propellor which is somewhat out of order: we kept under way until 4 o'clock when we anchored again near the Flag-ship.

The "Bermuda"— supply steamer— came in about 5 o'clock: from her we took (poor) potatoes and onions: the meat which she brought out had to be condemned, and was thrown overboard.

About 7 o'clock we returned to our station.

....

19

Began raining about 3 o'clock A.M. but it was but a shower, and at day-light it was all clear.

As soon as it was light enough we saw a double smoke stack steamer laying astern of the "Lackawanna" and a river (towboat) astern of the "Ossipee".

We got under way in the forenoon and went to the Flag-ship, found the strange steamers were both prizes to the "Lackawanna" – "Neptune", and "Planter", captured outside.

A year earlier, a slave named Charles Smalls, who functioned as ship captain of the Planter, strategized with the slave crew a way of escaping to the North. On a night when the Confederate officers went on shore at Charleston, Smalls donned the captain's hat to disguise himself and, knowing the proper signals to deliver, sailed the ship out of the harbor. The Planter stopped along the way to pick up family and friends and headed for the Union blockade. When they reached their destination, they raised a flag of truce and surrendered the ship to a very surprised Union fleet. The Planter must later have returned to Confederate hands.

We sent a Master's Mate on the "Neptune", and about 4 o'clock took the Eastwardly station.

....

21 SUNDAY—
Cloudy, rainy, uncomfortable. ship rolled very heavily all day. I came quite near being demolished in the forenoon—was writing at my desk a letter home—No. 27—when the ship rolling heavier than usual a large cake of ice on deck came down the hatchway.

I heard it coming and had just time to rise when it struck my side, two seconds sooner it would have struck me on the head, and if so would probably have killed me instantly.

Queer—that I should have gone through the last sixteen months and come so near death by a cake of ice after all.

Here is cause for thankfulness, and gratitude to God.

We changed our position after dark.

....

26
A very pleasant day. In the forenoon the Captain called me to the gangway and asked it I would like the position of Captain's Clerk?— I told him I did not know—he said the captain's Clerk on the "Aroostook" had gone home, and Captain Franklin had spoken to him, and he mentioned me, that he did not want to lose me, but I must decide for myself.

In the afternoon he sent for me to come into the cabin—when there he said he had been thinking over my position here and what it would be there: that there I would have many expenses, mess-bill, etc. and I could not lay up so much money as here.

To which I told him I know the expenses would be more, but I should have more to buy with.

He then said I would have much harder work - to which I said I should be satisfied to have as I did not learn enough here.

I then told him I disliked my position here very much indeed, and that I was compelled to associate with a class of men such as I had never associated with before, and hoped I never should again; that I would be sorry to leave the vessel, I had much rather say, but I would take any position, almost, so as to be relieved from mingling with such men.

He then said I would have unpleasant associates there—to which I replied it would be among a different class of men.

He seemed to wish me to remain but said, finally, that should Capt. Franklin speak to him again he would say I was willing to go— I told him yes.

I trust what will be done will be for the best, whether I go or remain here.

JUNE 27
Pleasant—warm—got under way after musters and went to the "Lackawanna" where we anchored all day. The Captain being on a court-martial command on board of her.

Returned to our station at night.

....

29
Pleasant and warm. Got under way at 9 o'clock and went to the "Lackawanna" on the court-martial.

Found the strange steamer which came in yesterday was the "Henry (Knitz")" from Key West, with prize crews of the blockading fleet off Texas.

The "Sam Houston" came in, either from Ship Island or the Passes, in the afternoon: brought news that the Rebels were, or had been in Pennsylvania— nothing more. Resumed our station before dark.

30
Pleasant and warm. The "Ossipee" came in early in the morning with a schooner which had tried to run in during the night. she was loaded with cigars and in general assorted cargo.

We got under way at 8 (...) - o'clock and went to the "Lackawanna" where the court-martial was being held.

We stopped there until 4 o'clock, when we got under way and went to the "Ossipee" and "Colorado" and then resumed our station.

....

(JULY) 2
Pleasant in the forenoon, and until about 4 o'clock when there arose a squall or wind and very little rain which did not last long.

We got under way at 8 (...) o'clock and proceeded to the "Lackawanna" to the court-martial.

The "Pocahontas" and "Aroostook" came from Pensacola bringing news that the "Union" had been there and started from there back north, not belonging to the Western Gulf Squadron.

By her I had a letter from Father of June 16, but whether my box came in (her) or not I do not know. She brought a relief to L.F. Wentworth, our Paymaster's Steward.

I am sorry he is going, for my own sake, but rejoice for him— and can only hope that my departure is not very far ahead.

We returned to our station before dark. The "Eugenie" went to Pass a l'Outre towing the prize captured by the "Ossipee".

3
Very pleasant and very warm. Got under way at 8 o'clock and went to the "Lackawanna" on the court-martial, remained there until 5 o'clock when we proceeded to the "Colorado" and our station.

From the "Colorado" the Ward Room obtained a paper of June 22 saying the southern army was invading the North.

JULY 4
Very pleasant. At 8 o'clock all the vessels in the fleet decorated with foreign E(nsigns) and signals, but not one of them showed an English or French flag.

The "Circassian" came from New Orleans early in the morning and we got under way and went to her. L.F. Wentworth, Paymaster's Steward, started for home in her: by him I sent a small bundle of citizens clothes and a letter home.

A salute was fired at 12 o'clock from the ship, and all the vessels in the fleet fired all their guns excepting their rifles.

We ran around among the vessels until 10 o'clock when we anchored near the "Lackawanna" until 18 h. when we anchored near the "Colorado" until 5 o'clock when we resumed our station.

I was not so homesick as last Fourth, but I felt somehat inclined that way—I did not receive any mail by the "Circassian", she bringing very little mail matter.

....

JULY 11
Pleasant—warm. Got under way in the morning and proceeded to –Lackawanna, anchored near noon by the "Colorado". The "Sam Houston" came from Ship Island in the morning with the news that Vicksburg was taken July 4, with 27,000 prisoners, and 200 guns,

and the "Kanawha" came from Pensacola bringing the reports there that Hooker and Lee had had a battle, that Lee was severely wounded, that Rosencrans had badly whipped Bragg in Tennessee capturing cannon, etc. etc.

Glorious news—hope it true-

Took Eastwardly station at 4 o'clock.

12

Pleasant—laid at anchor all day. no muster.

13

Very pleasant early in the morning but a squall of rain came up about 9 o'clock lasting a short time. The rest of the day pleasant.

We went to the "Lackawanna" in the morning: the Flag signalised that Port Hudson had been taken, and the Mississippi was clear. All the vessels hoisted their flags and (jack) forward, and at 12 o'clock fired a salute.

Resumed our station at night.

....

JULY 18

Very pleasant indeed. In the morning, soon after 12 o'clock the "Aroostook" made signal and sent up rockets showing that she had discovered a strange steamer. We repeated the signal and slipped our cable and stood in chase.

We could see the black smoke soon and the "Aroostook" continued firing and we right on chasing until daylight—soon after daylight we discovered the smoke and saw the "Ossipee" and "Aroostook" which were chasing also.

We had not chased long when we discovered another strange steamer standing across our bows, and she continued on that course for some time, we after her until she discovered us and altered her course.

We chased her all day, now gaining now losing, until after noon when we saw the "Ossipee" again coming into sight. We exchanged signals and kept on until dark—about 12 o'clock she was taken by the "Ossipee", and "De Soto" which had come up during the night.

It proved to be the "William Bagley" from Mobile with 700 bales of cotton - we then stood back in company with "Ossipee" and ("... ").

They captured the other steamers whose names I do not know.

JULY 19

We steamed along back all day and night, followed by the prize. We saw several sailing ships but spoke none of them.

It rained in showers several times during the day.

....

22

Took in provisions and stores and at 1 o'clock sailed.

Arrived at the blockade about dark. Saw two Rebel steamers out communicating with ours: found that one had sick and wounded prisoners from the (river), which they were handing over to the enemy.

Anchored Eastwards about 8 o'clock.

....

NEW ORLEANS (AUGUST) 20

Weather much the same as yesterday, alternate rain and shine. The Port Watch went "on liberty" in the mornoon for 48 hours. We laid still all day with (...) fires.

21
Very warm, and at night "millions of mosquitos"—no news—everything dull.

22
The time for which the Port Watch had liberty expires today at 10 o'clock. Most of them came off clean and sober, but several of them were dirty, noisy, and drunk.

23 SUNDAY –
I went on shore this forenoon with the Starboard watch on 48 hours liberty. The Dr.'s Steward and I were to (g...) all day. At first we went to the Custom house where the 26 Mass Reg. was quartered, from there to St. Charles Street where we found a friend of Lascombs and we stopped with him until noon, then had dinner at a dining saloon, then went out to the (Lake) where we stopped an hour, then returned on board.

24
Went on shore again this morning, got breakfast at a French Coffee House —had a dozen carte de visites taken, travelled around generally until 8 o'clock when returned on board.

....

28
Very pleasant and warm. I went on shore in the afternoon, to the Post Office, French Market, and down Canal Street and back on board.

29
Warm and pleasant all day. The firemen and engineers were at work all day on the shaft, and one mess went on shore on "Sundown liberty".

....

SEPT. 1
Very pleasant and warm. Work going on all day (unslipping) the propellor and the shaft. No news otherwise.

Took a strong dose of "Composition" at night, being unwell— and have been for several days.

....

6
Very warm indeed, but pleasant. Remained on board all day—had an opportunity to go on shore to church but did not feel able to go.

Was unwell all day.

SEPT. 7
Pleasant and warm. Remained on board all day. Unwell. No news.

8
Very warm and pleasant. Soon after 9 o'clock I went out on the levee to see a colored regiment reviewed by Maj. Gen. Banks, (...) Gen. Thomas, Brig.-Gen. Stone and other officers, then returned on board. Was quite unwell all the afternoon and night.

9
The "Columbia" came up from New York the 1st, at 10 o'clock last night. Do not know as yet whether she brought any mail or not.

I tendered my resignation as "yeoman" this morning to the Captain. To which he answered that Com. Bell would not consent for any one to leave the squadron. I told him that I had been unwell all summer, and that I did not feel able to do the duty now. To which he replied that my only course was to place myself under the Surgeon's survey.

And so the matter rests for the present only I hope: I trust that the way may soon be opened wherein I may bid adieu to the Navy forever, and welcomed to the pleasant associations of home.

10
The "Circassian" arrived during the night, and this morning I received a box in her from home. At noon Parks, the mail agent on board the "Circassian", came on board to see me, told me he saw Father and Mother the day they sailed: that they were well, and that he would gladly take any bundle or orders I might like to send.

Remained on board all day. No news. received a letter from Wentworth.

SEPT. 11
Somewhat cooler to-day than it has been since the first week we were here: there was a cool breeze all day.

At night we went to quarter of 1 bell and took clean hammocks so as to scrub the dirty ones in the morning.

We heard in the afternoon that the Texas Expedition proved a failure; that two gunboats were destroyed and the troops returned.

No arrivals—no news from North.

....

29
Raining all day and night. No news—yes—there was news of a great battle between Bragg and Rosencrans, but very few particulars.

Following two successful campaigns against the Confederates, Rosencrans was sorely defeated at Chickamauga, near Chattanooga. He was replaced after his defeat. The Union held Chattanooga, but food and supplies were diminishing as the city was virtually surrounded by the Confederates. By October 27, the Union was able to break through to Chattanooga with supplies.

....

OCT. 1
September has gone out, and October has come, "the all-golden month", when the leaves turn, and fade, and die.

I remember well one year ago this month on the blockade: the weather was very cool, as cool as we had it during the Winter, but the sea was smooth nearly all the month.

A good, cool breeze off land, causing us to remember the good, old New England weather we love so well.

Welcome October.

"Deal gently with us father Time."

Remained on board all day. No news (...) from up or down the river.

Quite cool all day—went on shore in the evening with Lascomb and Brown and got a plate of oysters.

....

4 SUNDAY—
Beautiful weather. For the first time for twenty months I went to church. In the forenoon I went on shore with (Mr. Go...ing), went to the Post Office, from there to a Methodist Church on Carondolet Street.

Very poor sermon from the text "Come unto me all ye that are weary (...)."

In the afternoon with Lascomb I went to the Cemeteries back of the city, or just outside the more settled portion.

From there we went to St. Charles Hotel where we stopped awhile and returned on board about 5 P.M.

The "Geo. Cromwell" and ("Mc Cle...") arrived from New York the 26th. I received no letter.

....

6
Very pleasant—sun shiny all day. We had reports in the evening that Rosencrans had been fighting with Bragg again, and that Bragg had been severely whipped. Have it prove true.

Remained on board all day.

See previous note on Rosencrans.

....

11 SUNDAY.
Warm, and pleasant. I remained on board all day. received a letter from (Maria) Sept. 30, about noon.

Another steamer came in during the night, but I do not know her name, nor where from. Heard by the mail that another captain (Lieunt) Com. McCann – was ordered to the "Kennebec", and that Capt. Russell was ordered North.

Hope it is true and that he will take me with him, if it is for the best.

....

22
Pleasant (sultry even then). Asked the Captain in the morning if he had ascertained as to carrying me home with him: told him I did not ask for myself, but they were so anxious at home. I wished to relieve their anxiety: to which he replied: "I assure you, Higgins, that I haven't forgotten you: I promised you I would do all I could for you. You had better let it alone."

Very satisfactory indeed. If he did keep his word I should be surprised, but I must say it is a mean idea to keep a person in suspense. Never mind; if he will get me home I will be satisfied. Remained on board all day. No news.

23
Commenced raining about daylight and rained all day. Grew cold towards night, and the evening was very cold and stormy.

Remained on board all day. No news of much interest.

Mr. (Wade) asked me in the forenoon if I would prefer having my discharge here, or wait for the "Circassian", allowing I could get it. I told him I would wait for the "Circassian".

24
Quite cool in the morning, and in fact, all day: cloudy with signs of rain. The Captain called me in the morning as I was walking up and down the deck and said that he had talked with Capt. Franklin, Fleet-Captain, and others and they have told him that he could not discharge me here: that my accounts had to go to a Navy Yard and be (un...ted), so he did not see what he could do: Captain Franklin told him it would be of no use for him to ask the Commodore, that he would refuse him.

I told him that it would be a great disappointment, not so much to me, although I had hoped to go, but to the folks at home who were expecting me every day.

He said – "I know—but they did not understand it"–

I told him I would like to have him ask the Commodore, and state to him that I could obtain a much better situation.

To which he replied that he would urge upon the Commodore and state that my necessities require me at home, but he thought the Commodore would refuse.

"All I can do then", he said, "is to see if I cannot get you discharged in Washington: I will go to Capt. (Wyman), Recruiting Officer, and I think he will order you home. He has the power to order any man home."

I then asked him if he thought there was any probability he would do it, and he replied that he thought he would.

So my dependence is in his remembering me when he arrives in Washington. I must remain on the "Kennebec" some time yet.

OCT. 25 SUNDAY
Cloudy in the morning and cold / grew warmer towards noon and night. Cloudy all day.

I went on shore about noon and walked through the city up to Carrolton: took steamer (...) – back, then went down to French Market, got a cup of coffee and piece of (pie)
....

28
Quite pleasant in the forenoon but in the afternoon clouded up and began to rain—did not rain very hard during the night.

The "Yazoo" came in from New York the 20th, during the night, brought word that Rosencrans was to be (supers...ded), which I do not believe, and that Lee had chased Meade to Alexandria, and Meade had driven him back to the Rapidan.

29
Rainy day—received a letter from Sarah in the forenoon, a Bangor paper, and *Harper's Magazine* for September and October.

OCT. 30
Alternate sunshine and rain all day, quite sultry, growing colder toward night. Did not go into the city.

The machinists finished their work in the afternoon, and the "cofferdam" was carried away.

Steamer "Continental" came down the river, bringing word that the Army of the Ohio, the Army of Tennessee, and the Army of the Cumberland had been merged into one called the Division of the Mississippi, that Gen. Grant had been placed in command, and that Maj. Gen. Sherman was to command the Army of Tennessee, and Thomas the Army of the Cumberland.

31
Early this morning Commodore (Bell) went past in a boat, and inquired why we were not out of (th...)? The Captain told him there was some difficulty with the shaft, and we had to be near the machine-shop. He ordered us to haul alongside the coal-wharf, and be ready for sea tomorow.

About noon a tow-boat came alongside, and towed us to the coal-wharf in (...)

In the afternoon I went around the place, but could see nothing interesting.

Coaled and painted, partially, in the afternoon, the majority of deck hands got drunk, and made the night hideous again, with noise.
....

NOV. 8 SUNDAY –
In the morning, before services, the weather was beautiful and was pleasant all day. But later it grew cooler and the wind blew hard from the N.W. It was quite smooth for vessels, but very rough for boats.

In the afternoon the "Circassian" came and in her came the new Capt. Captain Russell turned the ship over to him, mustered the crew, and said— "Men, as you all know, I have been (detached) and ordered home. I thank you for the assistance you have rendered me while we have been together. You have done well. You have behaved well–you have taken pride in the ships: I am glad to be able to turn you to my successor and say this." He then introduced him to the officers, and left.

The wind continued to increase while the boats were coming and going from the "Circassian"—it was dark by the time the Captain left, and boating was dangerous, and extremely difficult. We did not get all our boats hoisted until after 10 o'clock.

Capt. McCann remained on board the "Circassian" all night - about 10 o'clock we got under weigh and went to the N.E. to our station.

In the morning, at inspection of the (crew at) quarters, Capt. Russell told me he had seen the Commodore and he didn't see that he could do anything for me—that he would see the Secretary and Asst. Sec. of the Navy and see if he could get me home.

He has gone—was on board just twenty-one months. I hope we have made a change for the better. I trust we have made none for the worse.

I have no faith in any promise that Captain Russell made.

....

NOV. 15
Between 2 and 3 o'clock this morn a number of ("Eastern) lights" were found by the fleet and we got under weigh and stood out to sea: at daylight there was a schooner in sight, and the "Oneida" standing for her—we (t...d) towards both, and about 7 o'clock saw another in the distance nearer shore—chased. When we were near shore saw a party of horseman—stood in and fired, the "Oneida" firing first, (five times)—then stood out to sea— returned to station at 8 P.M. Pleasant and cool.

NOV. 16
This morning, about 9 o'clock the "Colorado" signalised this vessel 333—and we got under weigh and proceeded towards her—when we arrived within hail, the deck officer ordered us to "anchor near this ship, and send boats for provisions".

We ascertained that the "Bermuda" had been along yesterday while we were cruising, and left supplies on board the "Colorado" for us: likewise the "Jasmine" had been along from New Orleans but had no mail for us: I presume the letters are in the box in the New Orleans Post Office that we had while there. M.C. Wade—Ex-Off—was ordered to take command of the steamer "Gertrude" here, and a Mr. Baker was ordered here to take his place.

In the afternoon we went out fishing, but caught no fish—returned to our station soon after dark.

....

NOV. 25
Quite cold all day—but pleasant and (sun out): we did not get under way during the day, but in the night we got under way; and went out to a schooner which hove in sight, and came in collision with her through the stupidity of some one—not much damage done.

The "Arkansas" came from Pensacola in the afternoon.

NOV. 26 THANKSGIVING!

And away from home for the second time: last year at this time I hoped, and somewhat expected, should nothing happen, to be at home before this time, but here it is again, and home is as far off as ever.

We got under way in the morning after breakfast and ran down to Flag-ship and remained there all day.

I invited Lascomb and (Spaulding) to take some cake and pie. (pres...s) with me, so I had a much better dinner than last year Thanksgiving. I thought of home, much through the day—I wonder where I shall be next time the day comes (around).

....

NOV. 28

Cloudy this forenoon with the wind South East, which finally became rain at noon.

With the rain, the wind (hoved) to Northward, and it cleared away, partially before night. We got under way at daylight and anchored near the "Circassian" from which we received ice and one quarter fresh beef.

We sent three men on board the Sch. "M.C. (Lanfaire)" to repair her sails - and returned to our station at dark.

The "Circassian" left about 9 o'clock—for home—the "Oneida" gone to New Orleans.

NOV. 29

Sunday a pleasant, but cold day, the coldest we have had this season, with the wind from off land, and the water smooth.

We remained at anchor all day—a sloop came from West'd and kept on East'd in the afternoon.

We went to quarters and muster in the forenoon.

In the evening signals were burst, "enemy coming out", and the fleet got under way. Several guns were fired, either from Fort Morgan or the vessels; we ran around for some time, and seeing nothing, and all being quiet we returned to our station, and anchored about 10 o'clock.

....

DEC. 1

And the last month of 1863 has arrived, and it will very soon be 1864. This twelvth month came in pleasant, but cool, and, I hope, she will retain pleasant weather while she stops with us.

At daylight we could see the "Jasmine" from New Orleans, lying astern of the "Colorado", and at 10 o'cl. we went down—received a small mail, in which I had two letters and a paper—one letter from Chas. and a letter and paper from Sarah.

Ascertained that a schooner was captured on the night of the 29 when we got underway having on board 200 bales of cotton 20,000 in gold – etc., etc. – named the "Albert"—will be a prize to the fleet. Returned to our station after dark.

This ship was also known as the Wenona and its generous cargo rendered it an especially valuable prize (see Appendix D-10).

....

DEC. 7

Rough—wind N.E.—Ran out in the morning: at 10 went to Flag-Ship —sent us after the (guard) boat which had not been seen. cruised in and around (Sand) Island and offshore, found boat men nearly exhausted out at sea.

Anchored off main channel during night—"Bermuda" came in the evening.

....

DEC. 9

We went into Pensacola soon after daylight, and coaled and provisioned until dark.

On the way we fell in and captured the sch. "Marshall J. Smith" from Mobile with 260 bales of cotton, and put a prize crew on board—kept on and anchored within sight of the fleet.

DEC. 14

A beautiful day. quite mild, and very pleasant indeed, with the wind from off land.

We got under way about 9 o'clock and proceeded to the "Richmond"—when passing the Flag-ship she made signal—142—and we sent a boat on board for letters. I received one from Father, dated November 24—no papers. They came in the "Jasmine" last eve.

We laid at the Flag-ship until dark when we proceeded to our station.

Before anchoring the Flag-ship burnt our number, and 333. We went within hail, and the Commodore ordered us to go to the S.W. and see the steamer who was showing lights.

Proved to be the gun-boat "Pinola" from New Orleans. Returned to our station.

A beautiful evening.

DEC. 18

Today we exchanged men, sending the "Macedonians" on board the "Colorado" and receiving an equal number of men from her.

The Macedonia was a ship used for training new seamen. Higgins' use of the word "Macedonians" is unclear.

But they were all strangers, and, seeing our old crew go made me very homesick, more so than I have been for a long time.

O how I wish I may soon leave these associations!

How I wish I may soon, very soon, see home and the dear ones there.

We took the main channel station at dark.

DEC. 20 SUNDAY

A beautiful day—rather cool in the morning, but grew warmer as the day advanced and was very pleasant.

Went on shore about 10 o'clock and went down to Fort Barrancas: into the hospital burying ground, and around the soldier's quarters.

Had a good long walk with the Dr.'s Steward, Lascomb, came in this afternoon wrote a letter to Sarah: in the evening wrote one to (Dellie.)

I enjoyed the walking among the trees very much, and hope I shall be able to walk among more of them next summer.

DEC. 21

Very pleasant indeed all day. We took in stores: oiled the ship round: painted hammock cloths, etc. etc. sent boats on shore for repairs "and all that sort of thing".

DEC. 23

Very pleasant weather, and warm. We remained alongside the wharf all day and night. I went outside in the afternoon to the (stores) and back.

DEC. 24

We left Pensacola for the blockade about 4 o'clock, and reached here about 8 o'clock. The weather was quite unpleasant—and rough—we took station at the West'd.

DEC. 25 CHRISTMAS!

And a very dull Christmas too. I was on my back sea-sick all day, consequently it was not very enjoyable to me.

The weather was unpleasant, and it was so rough we could not communicate with the Flag-ship, so we laid at anchor. I felt somewhat better towards night, and before dark I took the (spar-deck) for it for several hours.

Did not sleep very well—and none at all the night before.

So Christmas Day was a dull day to me.

....

DEC. 30

Stormy—rough—uncomfortable—Very much so: the wind increased toward noon, and we anchored further from the bar with both anchors: the first time we had lain with both anchors down.

In the afternoon we weighed one anchor, and (s...d) by the other.

Very windy and unpleasant all day.

At night, between 7 and 8 o'clock, a steamer was discovered coming out, when we signalised, slipped and gave chase.

The "Genessee" also chased for a time; we ran to S.E. - all night, but saw no steamer.

I had a rough night of it—the water rolling around the berth-deck, rainy, rough and dark.

No sleep—no rest—no comfort.

DEC. 31

We continued the chase until about 9 o'clock a sail was reported off port-beam, and one off starboard bow.

We stood towards the one on the bow, which proved to be the Barque "Old Hickory" of Philadelphia, from there bound to New Orleans: she had lost her sails in a hurricane at 5 o'clock last evening.

We then went after the sail seen off the beam, which we could see was a fore and aft steamer standing to Westward.

We had no doubt she was the "Gennessee", cruising, like us in search of the prize and as we neared her she bore very much the appearance of her. We hoisted our number and the strange steamer hoisted a small American flag - but did not hoist any number—and she began to make a black smoke: we hoisted one jib and (fou...) and ran down to her, fired and she hauled down the flag.

With much difficulty, the sea being very rough—we sent a boat on board—and took charge of the steamer "Grey Jacket" from Mobile, with over 400 bales of cotton on board. Transferred her officers and men to us, and stood for Pensacola.

Made the light after dark and ran awhile and anchored until 12 when losing sight of the prize we got under weigh and stood to sea—made her again at daylight, and ran in to Pensacola

FRIDAY MORNING, JAN. 1, 1864

And here I will close this diary—whether I determine to keep another or not I cannot tell.

Two years are here—two years of the Past—What is in the Future?

Josiah Parker Higgins

(SECOND BOOK OF JOURNAL STARTS HERE.)
JOURNAL
SUNDAY, JAN. 3, 1864

JAN 3

A Diary is a bore: therefore this shall not be a diary.

A journal is better, but, I imagine, that this is rather borish too: yet I know, that, situated as I am, it is my duty to keep some kind of a record of the days as they glide along, so I will endeavor to heed this.

Then, to comence with, I am here, "Yeoman", on board this U.S. Gun-Boat "Kennebec"—Western Gulf Squadron — Division Blockading Mobile. Have held this unpleasant position nearly twenty-three months: how much longer I shall hold it this book may show.

It will be no easy thing to keep this as it should be kept: this to start with: there will be days of storm and roll, when it will be impossible to write, and, when such days are over many thoughts are forgotten.

Were it on shore it would be far easier, and much more pleasant in every way; but I am not on shore.

Then here goes to commence a new year: I trust I shall not be, as I am too prone to be, sentimental here, but hoping that it has blessings in store and happiness. Welcome 1864!

We left Pensacola yesterday forenoon, with the prize steamer "Grey Jacket", and reached here last evening.

WEDNESDAY MORN. JAN. 6 1864

Jan 6 It is very cold this morning, and last night was a very cold night—Yesterday was cold: the day before it rained all day. On Monday, the 4th, we recovered the starboard and chain—110 (faths) - which we slipped the night of the 29th when we went in pursuit of the prize steamer "Grey Jacket".

She went to New Orleans from here, Sunday forenoon, and in the afternoon the U.S. Gun - Boat "Port Royal" came from there, bringing a small mail of which I had one letter from Father, of December 17th.

The English sloop "Ajax" arrived here Monday, to communicate by flag of truce with Mobile.

Yesterday the "Octavia" arrived from Pensacola, and the "Port Royal" went to Pensacola during Monday night to replace smoke stack which was (disino...ted) Sunday night.

We got underway yesterday and anchored near Flag-ship returned to our station at dark. A new 1st Asst. Engineer reported for duty on board this vessel on Monday.

The second chapter of the "Kennebec" 's history commences this year: a new Captain, new Executive—new Engineer. Soon a new Paymaster, and probably (Surgeon), and a new crew—she will not seem like the same vessel.

1864 JAN 6

I took my "Quarterly Returns" into the Captain Monday P.M. and asked him if he had any objections to approving of my application for discharge?

He asked how long I had been in the service? Told him the 8th of next month would make twenty-four months.

He asked if I had been on the "Kennebec" all the time: told him yes, and that Captain Russell promised me that I should go home with him.

He said he did not know what right he had to promise that. Told him that I requested him to let me go in the spring of 63: that he was not willing I should go then: that when he received his orders he said I should go if the Commodore was willing: that when he went I was left. He replied that he "would see - probably do it".

Yesterday I handed my abstract of "Quarterly Returns" into E. Baker—Executive Officer: he wished them to be made out differently: took them into the Captain, he wanted something different, and so I went back and forth until I had made them over four times!

In my opinion neither of them know much about it - especially "E.B.", who, in my opinion, knows nothing.

SATURDAY MORN, JAN. 9 1864

On Wednesday night a boat was seen passing this vessel, and it was hailed, but no answer was made, so we slipped the chain and went after it.

It proved to be a boat with one man rowing in shore. He was ordered alongside, and he came on board.

He was a Mobile pilot, and when asked what he was doing outside he confessed that he had piloted a schooner out cotton laden: we signalised the Flag ship and gave chase after the schooner.

We ran all night S.E. and at daylight the weather was so very thick and foggy that we could see only the length of the vessel, but at 8 o'clock it cleared away a little, and a schooner was seen off starboard bow.

On seeing us she altered her course, and hauled on the wind. and finding that she was going very fast we made sail: the sch. seeing that we were gaining on her commenced throwing out cotton, and bale after bale went by us.

We fired at her several times from Parrot gun, but she was too far away to come near her, but we kept on, and she hove too just as we were training the x1 inch upon.

We ordered him to let his sails run down, and sent the gig and brought the men on board.

1864 JAN. 9, CONTINUED

A more desperate "black leg" set of men I never saw than came from her: they were all dressed in the best manner, and looked like a set of gamblers.

The sch. was named "John Scott", and was a beauty of a vessel—new, clean, clipper built, about 75 or 80 tons.

She had on board 110 bales—had thrown over 60 half bales. We took her in tow and ran until 7 o'clock P.M. when we signalised the Flag-ship and anchored.

The Mobile pilot who was captured rowing into shore was a very significant prize. It was recognized that his capture knocked a dent in the persistent and too-often successful blockade running, the John Scott being an example (see Commander Bell's two reports, Appendix D-11).

Yesterday evening we came to the Fleet, and laid there all day, taking our station at dark.

The "Itasca" came from New Orleans in the afternoon, and the "Colorado" sailed for the mouth of the Mississippi with the "John Scott" in tow at dark.

The "Itasca" brought a small mail, but I received nothing. I sent a letter—No. 53—to Father in the prize.

The weather for three days past has been very cold, wind off land. Wednesday it rained, but yesterday the (air there was) pleasant but cold.

The English sloop "Ferrgo" or "Verugo" — still remains here—communicated yesterday by flag-of-truce.

MONDAY EVE. JANUARY 11 1864
All day Saturday was spent foolishly, and, what the sailors call "humbugging".

Soon after daylight we got under way to recover the anchor we slipped to chase the "John Scott": we had been cruising around until about 8 o'clock when the "Albatross" came within hail and communicated that the Captain of the "Richmond"—Capt. Jenkins—wished us to follow him in, as there was a steamer on shore near Fort Morgan: so we followed the "Albatross".

The "Octavia" – "Pinola"– "Itasca" –"Gertrude" and "Albatross" with us steamed in and fired at intervals all day: the "Albatross" having the heaviest battery did more execution than all the rest, but none of us did her any injury that we could see.

After dark we and the "Albatross" went in and fired several times and then gave it up: during the night she was towed off and inside.

We laid still Saturday night – Yesterday we spent most of the forenoon in looking for the anchor, and not finding the bouy we ran down to the "Richmond" and anchored until nearly dark when we took a station to Eastward and guarding Swash Channel.

....

JAN 17
This has been a very pleasant day: warm, and sunny, mild as October. We had "Muster" at 10 o'clock, or just before, and the "Articles of War" were read by Executive.

I then went outside the yard to church for the second time since leaving home. The services were conducted according to the Episcopal forms by the Chaplain of the "Potomac", I think. He explained the parable of the first miracle of Christ, the one in Cana of making the water into wine.

In the afternoon, with Lascomb, I went to the colored regiment where church services were conducted by a colored man.

Afterward I returned on board.

The Flag-ship "Hartford", with Rear Admiral Farragut, came in from New York this morning, and is at anchor off the yard.

The "Pinola" sailed for the blockade last evening: the "Albatross" is here.

How I would rejoice to drop in on the folks at home to-night.

I hope I shall hear from them early this week.

JAN. 19
We spent the day yesterday in coaling, but did not finish. The "Hartford" went out in the forenoon, and Forts Pickens and Barrancas fired a salute to which the "Potomac" replied.

Homesick to-night, and good reason therefor.

A short time ago Acting Master Edward Baker of Plymouth, was ordered to this vessel, and became "Executive Officer."

He began on me the first day he took charge, and reprimanded me wrongfully.

For a few days I had been writing the ship log to oblige the then Executive Officer H.C. Wade.

When he left the vessel I thought it was not my duty to write it any more: and, according to Naval rules it was not my duty, and I did not write it for three or four days. The deck officer, supposing the log slate was copied erased the log each day for three days.

CONTINUED
JAN 19
And there I was not to blame as the slate was not erased they could see that it had not been copied.

But when "Acting Master Edward Baker" found that the log had been erased his wrath knew no bounds: he sent for me and told me that I had done wrong: that I had been accustomed to (write) the log —and there he lied— and that it was my duty, and there he confessed his ignorance of Naval rules.

So I wrote the log until Master Mate Nields returned.

Ever since this Baker has been in charge he has tried all possible means and ways to annoy and get me into trouble. Time after time has he done this without occasion.

I write this tonight because my mind is full of him, he having to-day again shown his spite. And I must say here that he is ignorant in all things appertaining to his duties, that, pretending to be religious, he is a hypocrite, and (a...ded ...) he is mean, (jealous), and selfish to the last degree.

How long it is destined for us to be together God only knows, but my prayer to Him to-night shall be that it will be as short as it can be consistent with His will.

JAN 19

I regret to take so much room in this book in speaking of so poor an object.

I regret to soil good paper in such a manner, but I shall feel better to free my mind in some way.

For about two years I have been away from home: I feel now that I should be glad should the occassion offer to leave this situation and services.

Come and come speedily is the wish of my heart.

Will it come!

Time—time only can tell.

FRIDAY EVENING, JAN 22, 1864

On the morning of Jan. 20, we came into the blockade: found here the Flag-ship "Hartford"– "Richmond" – "Oneida"– "Sebago"–"Port Royal" – "Octavia" – "Genessee" – "Pinola" – "Itasca" – "Gertrude" and "Penguin".

Mr. Butler returned from New Orleans, in the "Jasmine" which came in and left before we arrived.

He brought a mail in which I had two letters from Father.

....

By Father's letters I received word that Mary was dying. It came upon me unawares: the last news I had from her she was about to go out, and I had no idea she was so near death. Had I known that she was no nearly gone: had I thought that I should never see her again on the Earth I should have tried much harder to have gone home.

Perhaps it would have been of no avail; in that case I should have suffered much, but I would have tried with all my might.

The next news I expect to here is of her death. I would have liked to have been with her: I wish that I could have seen her again, but it was distined not to be.

I am thankful to God that He has been so kind, and that He has protected us so long from death.

May His mercy be extended still, and comfort and protect those who remain.

JAN 25

.......I am waiting anxiously to receive later news from home. I am confident that it will bring the sad intelligence of Mary's departure.

But, I know she has gone up higher, where she will suffer no more.

Heaven help me so to live that I may join her when my time shall come—for Christ's sake!

··

JAN. 27
..... The news from home is that Mary is failing all the time. I do not suppose she remains until this time.

All the family but Father were there when he wrote, Jan. 13.

May Our Father in Heaven watch over them.

Fort Morgan fired several rounds this afternoon, for practice I presume.

"Port Royal" returned from Pensacola..

JAN 30
..... I requested the executive, yesterday, to speak to Capt. McCann as to my going home: told him I would send home and get someone to take my place or do anything that he might think best, but that I get away.

I don't know as it will do any good, but I try, and if it is best. I trust the way may be opened whereby I can leave.

THURSDAY EVENING FEB. 4, 1864
The Executive informed me a day or two afterwards, Sunday I think it was, that he spoke to the Captain, who said he could do nothing, but that if I had some one to see the Secretary of the Navy he had no doubt but that I could get my discharge.

The same day I asked Paymaster Bennet if he thought it would do any good should I write to Captain Russell?

He said that there was no need of it: that Capt. McCann could discharge me on his own account and that he would speak to him.

A day or two afterward he informed me that he had spoken with him, and he guessed he would discharge me if I saw him and offered to get some one to take my place.

So yesterday afternoon I went into the cabin, and asked him if he would be willing to give me my discharge if I got someone to take my place?

"Who can you get?" he asked—I told him I would write home and get one—"I suppose he will be as green as you (was)"—he replied: I told him I was acquainted with the Paymaster's Clerk on the "Ohio", and would write to him.

"Well you get some one and I will give you your discharge." I sent a letter on board Flag-ship to day to home and to Wentworth.

FEB 4
I hope this will amount to something: I have tried for a long time to get this.

Sunday—Jan. 31—was a pleasant day: we had quarters, church services and muster. Since then we have been running around every night. Day before yesterday a steamer was seen ashore near the fort, so the heavy battery gun-boat went in and fired at her during the forenoon.

We also went in and fired several times, but she was too far within range of Fort Morgan for us to destroy her. The fort fired several times, the shots going outside of the vessels.

The same evening three deserters came off in a boat from the fort.

We have, for a few nights past been cruising near the shore to Eastward until lite, and are doing this now.

No mail from home since I wrote before.

SATURDAY EVE. FEB. 6, 1864
We were under way yesterday all day, and most of the night before, to the Eastward, going ahead slowly just enough to keep (head) to the sea.

Just before dark the "Sebago" went in towards the shore and fired upon a vessel on the reef. ......

I whitewashed—(holy-stoned), and cleaned my room, and spent several hours in the afternoon reading the poetry of (W.N. Prewel.)

The old Saturday night feeling is upon me, and I long for home—when shall I be there?

We are underway steaming to the Eastward.

....

FEB. 8

To-day is my birth-day and I am twenty-three! I can hardly realise that I have been so long in the world, and yet some period of it appears long when I look back.

Two years ago to-day I received my appointment as "Yeoman" of the "Kennebec" thinking to be in it not more than six or seven months.

Two years ago to-day the "Kennebec" went into commission, and I came on board: how well I remember it all!

Looking back the time, and the way seem long, and rough, and crooked, but I trust, I can see, now, a little straightening towards home.

I hope it will be so.

I hope the time soon will come when I can feel that I am indeed homeward bound.

There is much to be thankful for: preservation from death, from great dangers, and from violent sickness.

I would be grateful to my Heavenly Father for all His benefits in the Past: I would trust him for the future.

....

FEB. 11

If I was certain to-night that I was soon to leave all these associations and connections I should feel inexpressably happy, but doubts, fears and dread uncertainty will come over me in spite of all that I can do.

And when anything transpires to cause me to feel that I shall again be deceived, again so cruelly mocked, it worries me so much that I cannot sleep at night.

It seems a long, long time to look forward, and the days pass very, very drearily.

I wish that I could go to sleep and not wake up for six weeks: is this a wicked wish?

When I think how hard I have tried to get home: how much I have undergone: how long the time has been since I came away I become discontented and—I fear—peevish.

And yet how many have suffered more, infinitely more than I!

How many have given up their lives; what have I done that I should complain?

Nothing.

But I hope that this time I shall reach home.

It is the changes there that make me anxious.

God favor the Right!

SUNDAY MORN FEB. 14, 1864

We laid alongside the "Sebastopol" Thursday night, and Friday forenoon we hauled into the coal wharf, and, in the afternoon, we commenced coaling. Coaled until sunset, and finished Saturday forenoon.

In the afternoon took in stores and provisions, and we are now laying at the wharf with steam up.

Shall, probably, go out this afternoon.

The "Oneida" and "Octavia" went out last night, and the mortar schooners yester morning.

It is believed that Farragut will make an attack upon Mobile very soon.

He is here, but, report says, he will go to the blockade tomorrow.

There are some signs that he will be at work very soon, and, I hope we shall be aided by ironclads.

But there are none here now—they will be needed at Mobile as much as anywhere in my opinion.

If the contest is to come soon—may God assist, and defend the Right.

....

WED. MORN. FEB. 17, 1864
Yesterday the (ball) was opened. The mortar-boats commenced bombarding at Grants' Pass in the Sound.

Farragut's ships had difficulty with the shallow water of the area and he was further frustrated by the lack of land forces to assist him in the attacks on Forts Morgan and Gaines, which guarded Mobile. He was also concerned about the imminent presence of Confederate ironclads in the area (see Appendix D-12).

We could hear the reports, and see smoke, but could not tell what damage was done.

The wind was quite strong off shore, so we could not tell what they were shelling, probably a battery below Fort Gaines.

We changed anchorage both at morning and at night: but did not go a great way either time.

The "Albatross" came from New Orleans, and the "Sebago" from the sound.

Two or three small sailing vessels passed, bound to Pensacola during the day.

The "Albatross" came within hail in the evening, and her Captain came on board.

The mortars did not shell during the night, nor have we heard from them this morning.

Rather cool during the day but pleasant and smooth. quite cold in the night, more so towards morning.

Summary court-martial held on board on Poole and Welch for "absence without leave" – in the afternoon (muster) and sentence read – "loss of three months pay – 20 days double irons – on bread and water–"

....

FEB. 23
On Saturday last the new supply steamer "Admiral" arrived from New York, bringing us a new Surgeon and Paymaster and a Paymaster's Steward.

Dr. Perry left on her for New Orleans, the Paymaster remained to finish his accounts.

Lascomb, Dr. Perry's Steward, got all ready to go with him, but he went off and left him behind; he hopes to go when the steamer returns.

Sunday we remained at anchor, held church - services: at night ran inshore.

....

I have not heard direct from home later than Jan. 13; I know there must have been letters sent.

Nothing new as regards my going home: I fear that something will come to pass to prevent it, even should a relief come.

It seems to me that it will be thus as it has in the times past, and I do not allow myself to think upon the matter more than I can help.

Disappointed so many times: so many promises broken, I think I can trust no one. My heart's desire is to leave here, to get home once more: free; How sweet the word sounds and the term Citizen has a charm to me never known before.

I wonder how it sounded in the time of the French Revolution? It was used often enough, and I can imagine something of its power then.

It was great: it was might. But it has another significance to me, sweeter far.

But, I must believe it will come though it seems

"Exceeding slow"

....

FEB. 29

It is very warm to-day, and pleasant.

We are now at anchor near the "Richmond".

She came from Pensacola yesterday: the "Kanawha" came from New Orleans and went to Pensacola for coal: the "Jasmine" passed Saturday evening. We came down to the Flagship yesterday and received a mail. by which I had a letter from Father and Mother - Feb. 11, and one from Maria, Feb. 8.

Both contained the sad news that dear sister Mary died Jan. 31.

I have been expecting to hear it for several weeks but I was not prepared for it even then.

I can hardly believe that she has gone when I think of days gone by.

Provincetown will never seem the place to me that it has. I can never think of it now but in sadness.

She has gone—dear, gentle, sister Mary, gone forever!

Her memory is dear, and sacred.

May God pity them that remain, and assist them so to remember her that they shall join her by and bye.

....

MAR. 15

On Saturday last the tow-boat "Cowslip" came from New Orleans bringing our two officers who went there in the "Grey Jacket". She brought a mail by which I received a letter from Maria that had been in the New Orleans Post Office, "held for hostage", for some time.

It was dated Dec. 26, 1863. I also received one from her mailed Feb. 25, one from Vine – one from Suse, and one from Chas. same date.

Also some papers given to Chas. to send me by Wentworth.

Chas. wrote that he had been to see Wentworth, who said he could have sent one a few days before, but he would try to find some one soon.

I could have got Mr. (Ni..el's) brother to come had he known that I wanted a man: I wish I had known it when I wrote I would have had him here now.

However I trust I shall soon here that some one is on the way.

It makes me impatient to think of going oftentimes—I hope I shall not be again disappointed.

I wrote to Vine, Suse, Maria Sunday and sent the letters yesterday per "Jasmine".

We have had the Westerly station since coming from Pensacola.

....

MAR. 30

Last evening the captain sent for me on the quarter-deck: he was standing there with Baker - Ex - so called.

He asked me what I was doing as to my Quarterly Returns? Told him I intended to commence on them to-day: he wanted to know how long it would take to make them out? Told him three days: he then said you must make them out so as to have them in the morning of the 1st: told him I could not complete them until the morning of the 1st: said he knew it but <u>if I missed having them</u> in that morning he would order the Paymaster to keep half my pay if I (sho..) get my discharge at any time: this is "the gentlemany Capt. McCann"!

He also said write them plain so that I can read them: you write so that I cannot read more than half—I had a mind to tell him that he did very well, but I have no wish to be court-martialed, and I know he would not hesitate to do this—if he deemed that I was in the least trifling with him. So I lit a light, and worked on my returns until 11 o'clock, and have been at them all day to day.

I seem to be fated: I have used every man and officer on board the "Kennebec" as well as I knew how: for twenty months I got along without a cross (...) from my commanding officer, and since then I have never received a pleasant one from the Ex -

He has poisoned the mind of the captain against me. I have no friend to take my part, and must fight it out alone.

With my affliction to bear, I think it is rather hard—I can only trust in God—I would believe that He watches over me.

THURS. AFTERNOON, MAR. 31, 1864
What kind of a Journal is this that I am keeping here? A very poor kind indeed, I think: neither one thing nor another.

But it must (ru...) along—how long I wish I knew.

It was my firm intention when I began this that it should not be a book of complaints, but I fear it is hardly anything better. I can realise what a journal should be: I can appreciate a good one when I see extracts from it, but keeping it myself, this is a difficult matter. I must confess that there has been quite a change in my ideas of this matter since four years ago: I don't think it is such a (dis...turn) as it was then.

However this is no pretention towards a journal: it shall not go under that name.

Dots—how will that do I wonder?

Murmurings—I think that would do better.

We are at anchor away to the Eastward, out of sight of the fleet: have been cruising around all the forenoon.

SATURDAY FORENOON, APRIL 2, 1864
We laid at anchor out of sight of the fleet but a short time on the 31st when we got under way again and ran further inshore.

Anchored a long distance from the shore: the "Jasmine" came from New Orleans in the afternoon and went to Pensacola.

The "Pembina" brought a mail to us from her just before night by which I received a letter from Father—Mar. 17—and one from Vine—Mar. 16.

It was very rough towards night and during the night, the wind being S.E. and there being a very heavy swell rolling in from the gulf.

We got under way yester forenoon and went to the "Oneida"—Flag-ship where we laid until night when we resumed our station.

I took in my "Quarterly Returns" yester forenoon and asked Capt. MCann what I had done to incur his displeasure? He said that I had not incurred his displeasure, but I did not seem to take any interest. I told him I had always tried to do all my duty: that for twenty months I did not receive a cross and that since then I had not rec' a pleasant one—said that was nothing to him—told him the treatment I have (...) from Ex - and he said that when I got a relief I could go home.

How can I get a relief? This is the question: Father writes me that he can get no pass for a man to come down even if he gets a man to come. And there it is.

Red tape! Red tape!

Yesterday I wrote a note to N.M. Dyer asking him if he thought he could get a man in New Orleans, but I do not expect to hear any thing from it.

I want to get out of this very, very much: I don't want to stop until another quarter has expired.

It is misery to me under existing circumstances.

I had rather serve my country in some other capacity then as yeoman of the "Kennebec".

When I think of home it seems to me that I cannot remain here, but it may be my duty.

I trust that I shall be guided aright by Him who knowth all things. "All the paths of the Lord are mercy and truth unto such as keep His covenants and His testimonies"

I would keep them with my whole heart.

TUESDAY MORN, APRIL 5, 1864
.... There has been but six vessels on the blockade for a day past, and night before last (Swash) Channel was not blockaded.

Consistency –

When there was a moon there were eleven vessels here: now, when the nights are dark, there are but six!

The "Eugenie" came from Pensacola yesterday and went to New Orleans.

Admiral Farragut went to New Orleans in the "Tennessee", passing here Sat. night as we were coming from fishing banks.

No news.

Weather, at present, beautiful –

WED. EVE. APRIL 6, 1864
.... As I look at the trees on shore it makes me more discontented and home-sick than ever: they look so quiet, peaceful, and resting. O how much I wish I would spend the summer months in Maine!

APR. 12
We still lay at the yard undergoing repairs on vessel and engine: caulking etc. etc. The crew have been on shore on liberty, and, as usual, came back drunk, most of them in fighting trim.

We finished coaling Thursday, and Friday one watch, rather Saturday, one watch went on shore on twenty-four hours liberty.

Sunday I went to church in the forenoon, and in the afternoon went into the woods, a short distance......

THURSDAY, APRIL 21, 1864
The supply steamer "Admiral" came from the Westward late Tuesday afternoon, and from her we received supplies and a mail. I received four letters: one from Chas: one from Marie: one from Sarah, and one from Vine.

Marie wrote that (dear) little Charley Cook had gone to his Mother: died with scarlet fever and (throatail).

Poor gentle Soul: I loved him much: it pains me to think he has gone, but it must be better thus. I feared for him when I thought of him growing up in this wicked world: but he is safe now.

Mother and son together—I think the Father will soon join them.

All these changes make me the more anxious to get home, but I see no chance for it right away. I shall keep on trying all I can to get there, and trust in God.

We went fishing yesterday, and at night resumed our station. The "Oneida" went to Pensacola—and the "Ossipee" is Flag-ship.

Weather very pleasant –

TUESDAY, APRIL 26, 1864.......
..... On Sunday I wrote to Rear Admiral D.G. Farragut, applying for my discharge.

Capt. McCann kindly approved of it, and it was sent on board the "Ossipee" the same day to await steamer to New Orleans. I stated to him just how I was situated, and my reasons for applying.

If this fails I do not know what more I can do: I have tried, and tried again: this seems my last resource.

I hope, and trust, and pray, that this may be successful. I want to get home as soon as possible.

....

MAY 14 .....
..... On Tuesday evening I sent down word to Capt. McCann that I would like to see him—he sent back and asked if I wanted any thing important! I answered—yes—he sent back wanting to know if it was connected with my duty! I sent word—No—to ask a favor—he replied that he was busy—would see me some other time.

Yester noon he sent for me—wanted to know what I wanted the other day! Told him I wished to ask him if he was willing to give me the appointment of "Yeoman", (...) so that I could send it home, and get a man to come out—said that wouldn't do—he couldn't tell what sort of a man would come, might be a man he wouldn't have on board the ship—told him I thought of going to Capt. Drayton—with his permission—said he didn't care how much I saw him —for his part he wished I could get my discharge and clear out—told him I had done all in my power—Said he would see if he could do anyting and not commit himself—when he saw Capt. Drayton he might speak to him about it.

I have tried all I know to get away and seems as far from it now as ever.

THURSDAY MAY 19, 1864
We are still at the navy-yard repairing: in the dock with us are the "Port Royal" - "Pinola" - "Jasmine" and "Buckthorne".

The "Glasgow" went out last night—the "De Soto" came in yesterday: the "Seminole" and "Nightengale" went out, and the "Tennessee". We have news that a great battle has been fought in Virginia, but we have no particulars, and know not the result.

I trust we shall hear full reports this week.

The weather is pleasant and very warm.

I get no nearer home than ever: I have been intending to go on board the "Hartford" and see Fleet Captain Drayton, but have not the slightest idea it will be productive of any good—I will go and see, however, when an opportunity offers.

It is hard to remain here all through this hot summer when I have been here so long. I think that I deserve to go now, and I can not bear to think that I must stop, but I must bring my mind to it.

It is hard—hard—hard, but it may be for the best.

"A good man's steps are ordered of the Lord"—if I could believe that I was thus guided I would be far more content.

MONDAY, MAY 23, 1864.....
.....We know that there has been terrible fighting, still going on at last accounts, but know nothing later than May 14.

The "Penguin", from Key West, came in Saturday.

The "Albatross" left for home yesternoon, by whom I sent a letter home.

....

SUNDAY, MAY 29, 1864
On the passage from Pensacola to the fleet, with the blockade in sight; we sailed from Pensacola last night and have been cruising around. The "Oneida" and "Tennessee" also sailed from there last night, and the "Cornubia" arrived there before we left.

We coaled yesterday the balance left from the day before, and left, as usual, "all up in a hup". Farragut is on the blackade here with a larger fleet than usual on account of the ram "Tennessee".

WED. EVE. JUNE 1, 1864
We have been stationed at the Eastward since coming from Pensacola—last night we had general quarters, got underway, and ran out to sea: returned this morning, and this forenoon all the fleet were under way going through the maneuvering of an engagement.

I do not know whether there will be an attack soon or not: my opinion is not, but there were never so many vessels here at one time before—but they are all wooden.

"Hartford" – "Richmond" – "Brooklyn" – "Ossipee" – "Seminole" – "Lackawanna" – "Oneida" – "Monongahela" – "Galena" – "Metacomet" – "Genessee" – "Tennessee" – "Kennebec" – "Pinola" – "Pembina" and "Penguin"—the "Itasca" – "Port Royal" – "Cornubia" are in Pensacola.

TUESDAY, JUNE 7, 1864
We ran into the "Port Royal" night before last while communicating with her, carrying away our 1st cutter and gig.

We got underway and went to general-quarters about 2 o'clock. Signals being made that a steamer was running in: we kept under way all night and stood for the fleet again at daylight: Soon after the "Metacomet" came in with a prize-side - wide wheel steamer, loaded with arms and ammunition, bound in......

....

JUNE 21 NAVY YARD, PENSACOLA, FLA.
We came in here Sat. morn.

Hauled into the dock this morning—shall probably be here ten days, under going repairs on boilers.

It has rained every day since we came in, showers, sprinkles now. In here are "Richmond" – "Lackawanna", "Metacomet", "Cornubine", "Cowslip", "Narcissus", "Conemaugh", and the usual sailing ships stationed here.

"Eugenie" – "Glasgow" – went out this morning.

....

THURSDAY AFTERNOON, JUNE 23, 1864
Yesterday was pleasant all day.

The "Lackawanna" went out in the forenoon for the blockade.

Carpenters were at work on board repairing starboard waist hammock netting damaged by running into the "Port Royal".

In the forenoon I overhauled one of the shelves in the storeroom "putting every thing to right".

My afternoon work did not amount to much—can't remember what I did, conclusive proof that it was of no account.

The days do not slip away so quickly here as they do blockading, and I realize more keenly how many hours I waste.

One thing I have no books for proper study: another thing I have no inclination: every thing here seems unnatural, and is.

Humbugging a plenty is going on here under this administration, and ever will be I can see.

If ever a poor unfortunate would "jump for joy and also sing" it was be the individual writing this to know that he was once more his own master—(free) –

I went into the water last eve with Lascomb—had a good bath.

FRIDAY AFTERNOON, JUNE 24, 1864

We laid at the wharf yesterday until 7 o'clock, when we hauled across the dock and alongside the "Cornubia", to allow the "Metacomet" to coal.

In the forenoon I drew of half a barrel of oil and put into tank: the afternoon cool spent in one way and another, a part of it in reading "Bitter Sweet".

A very good sermon, and poem. I wrote sermon entirely unconsciously, but it will well apply—and contains several fine passages, and descriptions.

Of course I read passages from the Book above, and beyond. All other books—chapters in (Joshua), Eccl - and Acts.

If ever I have the opportunity I shall highly prize reading with a commentary. I wish I could now.

I wish I had more good book-poetry-history-travel etc. it would be a good study for me.

The "Circassian" came in, from New Orleans, last evening: I waited upon deck some time after a boat had gone on board to see if she brought news of mail—the boat returned, and, hearing nothing I "turned in".

FRIDAY AFTERNOON, JULY 1, 1864

We are still in Pensacola, but off the Navy Yard, and in the stream: we were towed out by the "Jasmine" night before last.

My last entry was one week ago this morning: that forenoon I was surprised to learn from Paymaster Marker that there was a Dr. Boyden on board the "Circassian" who inquired after me and wished me to come on board.

Inquiring I heard that she was to sail at 10 o'clock, as the commodore would not allow her to coal here, there being but little on hand.

I went on board and saw him about twenty minutes, and at 1 o'clock went on board again and saw him, and at 4 o'clock she hauled alongside the wharf, and that evening Boyden came on board.

I went on board the "Circassian" the next day and saw him, and that evening he came on board again.

The day after—Sunday—I was on board there, and he here, and Monday I was on board. That day Lascomb went on board to take passage, by permission of the Dr. and Capt.

Tuesday eve she hauled from the wharf: the following morning went to sea.

I am very glad that I saw Boyden: he is going home on one month's leave.

I was sorry to have Lascomb leave for my own sake—glad for his.

Monday Captain McCann told me to make an application to him for my discharge and he would enclose it in a letter to the Admiral requesting it: I did so, and await the time when we shall go on the blockade.

I should have highly enjoyed going on the "Circassian" with Boyden and Lascomb, but shall esteem it a great privelege to go on the next boat that goes if I have it.

It seems to me doubtful, but I hope to go.

SAT. AFTERNOON, JULY 2, 1864

Turned in last night on deck, under the starry sky, about 8 h o'clock, and laid somewhat uneasily, until 4 o'clock this morning.

Turned out and entered upon the duties of another day.

Saw the "Circassian" – "Bermuda" – coming in soon after daylight: she anchored alongside the wharf.

It made me very anxious, to see her coming in and think of her going home again in two weeks: Somehow the more I think upon it the more it seems that the Admiral either will pay no attention to my application or he will answer nay—It seems so but I hope not. Weather yesterday was very pleasant and warm: did not do much of any thing.

Plenty work on hand to-day. It is Yeoman this and Yeoman that, and this has been the cry, so far, all day........

SUNDAY AFTERNOON, JULY 3, 1864

Here we are back again on the Mobile blockade: have just come to an anchor, and the gig is now on the way to the "Hartford". (I that) she might return with the welcome news — "Yeoman go home".

We started fires last eve, came out about 8 h o'clock, and ran S.E. I suppose from the course we were steering this morning.

We had quarters and muster this morning, and the "Articles of War" read in an indistinct, hum drum, monotonous tone by the Ex.

Weather very warm and pleasant.

We saw the "Metacomet" firing at a vessel on the beach, near the fort, as we came in.

TUESDAY AFTERNOON, JULY 5, 1864

The night of the 3rd the "Itasca", "Pembina" and we went in and fired on the vessel on shore and humbugged around all night.

We fired several times, and the fire was returned from the shore: two shots went over us, and the "Pembina" was struck once.

Yesterday morning we ran to the Flag ship and laid all day, dressed ship, and at meridian all the vessels fired a salute.

In the afternoon the "Galena", "Oneida", "Monongahela", "Genessee" and "Lackawanna" ran in and fired, and the Admiral ran in on the "Cowslip" - no damage done.

At night we and the "Port Royal" went in again, and were at quarters all night firing several times.

This morning came down to Flag-ship where we now are.

Soon after the salutes were fired the messenger-boy told me Mr. Baker wanted me: I went there and he read me the answer to my application to the Admiral.

"Sir –
Presuming from your letter that you can dispense with the services of Yeoman Higgins you will discharge him and send him North when you have supplied his place.
D.G. Farragut
Rear Admiral"

I felt very much disheartened before I heard this, very much so indeed, after it felt better—much better.

The "Bermuda" went from here yesterday: a man might be given me to learn to take my place, and I could go on her as easily as could be, but this delaying, putting off, will, I fear cheat me of it.

I should like to go very much. I would get home in time to go down East if every thing was right, whereas, if I wait it will make it too late.

I can only wait and hope.

WED. M. JULY 6, 1864
Again, and for the third night, we went in near the Rebel Steamer on shore, this time towing in two boats, and armed crews, from the "Hartford" the "Metacomet" also went in towing two boats.

It lightened visibility early in the night, but this passed off before midnight.

We ran in very near the shore and steamer several times, and about 12 o'clock the boats from the "Metacomet" and us started in, boarded the steamer, and set her on fire returning safely to both ships.

Muskets were fired from the shore but no one was injured and we towed the boats to Flag-ship. It was very well done indeed: we were within sight of the fort and in close to a battery, but they did not fire upon us.

Just before dark the "Glasgow" came in from New Orleans, and we received a mail. I a letter from Suse and one from Vine – No. 8 –

I hear nothing more of going home: nothing is being done, no man picked out to take my place: one might be chosen and I learn him his duty and be ready to go on the "Bermuda", but I must wait their time. May it come very soon.

FRIDAY, P.M., JULY 8, 1864
Yestermorning early we got under way as usual and ran down to near Flag-ship and anchored: all the fleet have done this since the Admiral has been here.

Laid quietly all day, and last night we took an Easterly station again, and laid quietly all night......

.....Nothing new regarding my going home, nothing has been done or is being done to get a man to relieve me, and, I think they do not care to who have the power.

There is a report this morning that there is a Monitor now in Pensacola, the "Manhattan"—I hope it is so, one is needed here very much.

TUES. MORN. JULY 12, 1864
Last Saturday morning before I "turned out" the messenger-boy called me, saying Mr. Baker wanted me—turned out and went on deck. Mr. Baker and Capt. McCann aft. Mr. B. said—"Yeoman—you will turn over your books to Cornelius (Lancum), and be ready to go home in the 'Bermuda' ".

With a glad heart I returned forward. Sunday morning another steamer was ashore on the beach near Fort Morgan. during the day several steamers went in and fired upon her, and we were in there all Sunday night. Yesterday afternoon we and the "Pinola" went in and fired at her for several hours, and took an easterly station at night.

I believe she got off last night and went in.

We hear that there are two monitors in New Orleans.

Have not commenced to pack up yet as I am waiting to get a box from Paymaster Steward. hope to get it this morning and be ready and see the "Bermuda" tomorrow or next day.

Weather warm – pleasant –

Higgins was discharged from the Navy at this point. In the original diary, the next page has only "As Citizen" written in the center. Included as the final entry in the transcription is the first entry in the "As Citizen" section, recounting his return home.

(NO DATE)
I left the "Kennebec" July 16 on the supply steamer "Bermuda", and arrived at Philadelphia on the morning of July 26.

The passage home was pleasant, except three days off Hatteras, where we had it stormy and rough: we touched at Tortugas— Port Royal and Hampton Road.

I left Philadelphia the same day at 11 A.M. in the cars for New York: arrived there about 3 o'clock P.M. Took the Fall River boat at 5 o'clock, arrived in Fall River the following morning at 5 o'clock, took the cars for Boston, arriving at 7.30.

Took coach at the Depot for home, through East Boston, found the house closed and folks all absent: went to the store, saw Father, said Mother, Maria, and Susan were in Dexter.

Vine was to go with them, but by some means was left; where she was he did not know, but he went directly to East Boston to find out, from there to the city and to Cambridge (pass), but could find nothing of her.

Marshall and family had gone down East, he going with them as far as Portland: he thought likely she had gone with him.

Early the next morning—July 28, Father went to East Boston again: saw Vine: she did go down and returned with Marshall. Father then came home and about 9 o'clock I went over and thus saw her first after being separated thirty three months.

Having many errands to do for persons on the "Kennebec"—I left E.B. about 10 o'clock, returned home, and going to the city called upon several that I had promised: saw Marshall at the market; went with him to the "G. Shattuck", saw Porter, and while there Vine came down, and we three—went to 11 Vernon St. and took supper: there saw Mrs. G.A.A.

In the evening went with Marshall and Vine to the E.B. ferry, then came home.....

....

POSTSCRIPT

At dawn on August 5, three weeks after Higgins left the Kennebec, the fleet engaged in the battle of Mobile Bay. A notoriously bloody battle, it was over within three hours. The Confederates had brought in as their ultimate weapon the ironclad Tennessee, only to have it repeatedly rammed by the Hartford under Farragut's command. With the surrender of the Tennessee, access to this major port city was shut off to the South. After Fort Gaines and Fort Morgan surrendered, the Kennebec assumed blockade duty along the coast of Texas until the end of the war. Near Galveston she participated in one of the final Civil War activities with the destruction and burning of the captured Denbigh.

The Civil War came to an end on April 9, 1865 when Lee surrendered to Grant at Appomattox Court House, Virginia. The formal ceremony took place on April 12. On April 14, Good Friday, President Lincoln was shot at Ford's Theatre in Washington. He died early on April 15.

The Kennebec was assigned to the Texas coast as a Union presence until July, 1865, at which time she headed home, returning to Boston on August 1. She was decommissioned and sold on November 30 of the same year. *

Following the battle at Mobile Bay, the Hartford was decommissioned while it underwent repairs, after which she joined the Asiatic Station Squadron as flagship until 1875. She sailed again as flagship of the North Atlantic Station in 1882, then was stationed in the Pacific until decommissioned in California in January 1887.

Continuing her history of active service, the Hartford was recommissioned and transferred to the Atlantic as a training ship in 1899. She was reassigned to Charleston from 1912 until decommissioned in 1926. In 1945 she was towed to the Norfolk Navy Yard, where she sank in 1956. **

David Glasgow Farragut, born in the South and raised after his mother's death by the family of well-known naval officer, David Porter, claimed Union loyalty at the outbreak of the Civil War. He was nearly sixty when he assumed responsibility for the West Gulf Blockading Squadron. Following the war he retired to New York City where he died six years later on August 14, 1870.

Within a short time of Higgins' return home, he married Lavina Adams, who lived only a few years. He was appointed to a position of state-wide church superintendent in Maine and then became a merchant for much of the rest of his life in Massachusetts. After Lavina's death, Higgins married a Florinda Goodwin of Maine, who survived him, drawing a pension on his Civil War service. Higgins died suddenly at Hyde Park, Massachusetts in 1895.

Anonymous, Dictionary of American Naval Fighting Ships, Volume III, p. 618-619.

**Ibid, pp. 261-263.*

APPENDIX A

Chronological list of ships mentioned from unedited journal

Augusta Norwood
Judah (Conf.)
Kennebec
Rhode Island
Hartford
Brooklyn
Mississippi
Itasca
Winona
Oneida
Kineo
Iroquois
Nightengale (Yusuf)
Harriet Lane
Verona
Wissahecan
Sciota
Pensacola
Richmond
Portsmouth
Penola
Katahdin
Caingu
Rosalie
Anglo-American
Tennessee
Cayuga
Neville
Acorn
Susquehannah
Preble
Kanawha
Bohio
Ocean Queen
Star (Conf.)
Connecticut
Unitas
R. R. Cuyler
Union
Lackawanna
Colorado
Autumn Queen
Sam Houston
Bienville
Charles Henry
Pocahontas
Geo. Peabody
Antona
Gen. Washington
Rocky Hill
Pelican of New Orleans
Potomac
W.S. Anderson
Circassian
Anthem
W. Hunter
Aroostook
Pembina
Gen. Banks
Alex Milliken
Juniper (Conf.)
Mary Magdalene
Independence
Continental
Columbia
Canada
United States
Morning Star
Magnolia
Bermuda (Thames/Thomas)
Ossipee
Eugenie
Wm. Wilson
Princess Royal
Sea Lark of Boston
Neptune (Conf.)
Planter (Conf.)
Henry (Knitz)
De Soto
William Bagley (Conf.)
Bay States
Unida
St. Mary
Morgan
Jasmine
Enchantress
Crescent
Jackson
Evening Star
Champion
Thomas A. Scott
Creole
Locust Point
Geo. (Cromwell)
McCle...
Yazoo
Genesee
Gertrude
Port Royal
Albatross
Octavia (Sisyoo)
Arkansas
M.C. Lanfaire
Alert (Conf.)
Marshall J. Smith (Conf.)
Penguin
Old Hickory
Grey Jacket (Conf.)
Ajax
John Scott (Conf.)
Gertrude
Chas. Frost of Philadelphia
United States of New York
Champion
Sebastopol
Sebago
Admiral
Metacomet
Glasgow
Cowslip
Conemaugh
Clyde
Rachel Seaman
Seminole
Hendrick Hudson
Buckthorne
Galena (an ironclad)
Cornubia (Nell)
Narcissus
Manhattan (an ironclad)
Monongahela

APPENDIX B
Chronologic list of names of military personnel

Capt. Higgens
Capt. Russell
First Lieut. Blake
Brid. Gen. Duncan
Brid. Gen. Williams
Gen. McClennan (sic)
Beauregard
Jeff Davis
Foote
Rear Adm. Farragut
Commodore Smith
Van Dorn
"Stonewall" Jackson
Grant
Wm Brooks, Ex. Off.
  (died on "Magnolia")
Capt. Franklin
L.F. Wentworth,
  Paymaster's Steward
Hooker
Lee
Rosencrans
Bragg
Com. Bell
Maj. Gen. Banks
Gen. Thomas
Brig. Gen. Stone
Morris
Mail Agent Parks
Capt. Wyman, recruiting officer
Meade
Sherman
M.C. Wade, Ex. Off.
engineer Robinson
Dr. Perry
Lascomb, Perry's Steward
Capt. McCann
Spaulding
Edward Baker, Ex. Off.
Master Mate Nields
Paymaster Bennett
Poole and Welch, court-martialed,
  with "loss of 3-mos.pay, 20 days in
  double irons - on water and bread."
Capt. Drayton
Dr. Boyden

APPENDIX C
Reading material received by mail

Atlantic
Boston Traveler
Harper's
Time-Weekly Tribune
Bangor, Maine newspaper
Chelsea, Massachusetts newspaper

APPENDIX D-1A
(Report of Farragut to Gideon Welles, Secretary of the Navy, regarding the unfortunate results of French Captain Cloué's expedition up the Mississippi River)

U.S. FLAGSHIP HARTFORD
MISSISSIPPI RIVER, HEAD OF THE PASSES,
APRIL 11, 1862

Sir: I have to inform the Department that H.I.M.S. Milan arrived here on the 6th instant. Captain Cloué requested permission to communicate with his consul by telegraph from Fort Jackson, to which I readily consented, and offered him the services of one of the gunboats to tow his boat up to within 3 or 4 miles of the fort, which he accepted, but desired that she should not go too near the fort, as he did not wish to compromise his own neutral character, or myself, by going near enough for observation.

I, accordingly, on the morning of the 8th, gave the captain a pass and sent the commanding officer of our advance station (about 5 miles below the forts) a special note to let the captain pass. He passed up with the gunboat Winona, Lieutenant Commanding Nichols, and when they arrived at the advance station...Nichols informed Commander Boggs, the commanding officer, of his orders. The latter directed him to hoist a flag of truce, to which...Nichols replied that the flag-officer had given him no such orders, but simply to tow the boat to within 2 or 3 miles of the fort. Commander [Boggs], however, insisted that so long as the French captain remained with him he would hoist the flag of truce. Captain Cloué, by this order, was made very uncomfortable, and in a short time left the vessel in his boat and pulled up for the fort. ...Nichols hauled down his flag and returned to the advance post.

In the meantime... Boggs had come down the river to have some repairs made, and Commander De Camp had become the senior officer; ordered... Nichols to take him back to the fort and to hoist a flag of truce, saying he was determined to catch that Frenchman and not permit him to go up.... Nichols remonstrated with him against his proceeding, told him that the captain had my pass to go to the forts to telegraph to his consul, and tried by every means in his power to deter [De Camp] from proceeding, but to no effect. So soon as the vessel arrived within the line of fire, the fort fired a blank cartridge and... Nichols insisted upon stopping. Commander De Camp then got into his boat and continued to pull up when they fired a shot over him. He then stopped, and a rebel steamer with a flag of truce came out to him, and he went alongside of her. Soon afterwards he left the rebel steamer with Lieutenant John Wilkinson, formerly of the U.S. Navy, an army officer, and a civilian, and took them on board the Winona, where he showed them the battery of said vessel and told them who commanded here. They remained on board the Winona upward of an hour, and informed him in return that they had just gained a great victory over us at Corinth, in which we had sustained a total defeat and lost four generals and many thousands of men, all our gunboats, etc. The rebel officers finally made the move to depart, themselves, and... Nichols returned and made me the above report.

The next morning Captain Cloué returned on board in his boat, full of chagrin and mortification, and informed me that, in consequence of the movement of the flag of truce by Winona, he had been imprisoned, and kept so until a few hours before, when he was permitted to depart. As the rebels insisted upon it that it was through his means that our vessels had come up and made their observations and caused them to lose a steamer, which they had run ashore and burned, being outside of the chain, and not observing the flag of truce hoisted on the vessel, they believed that they would be captured, so set fire to the vessel and fled to the shore. I expressed to Captain Cloué my deep mortification that he should have suffered such inconvenience from the misconduct of any officer under my command, but that I had already had the officer relieved and instituted a military investigation of his conduct, the proceedings of which I have the honor to enclose herewith.

Very respectfully, your obedient servant,
D.G. Farragut
Flag Officer Western Gulf Blockading Squadron

(Stewart, Official Records...,Series I, Volume 18, pp. 112, 113.)

APPENDIX D-1B
(Letter to Commander DeCamp from Farragut re: enquiry into incident with French Captain Cloué)

HEAD OF (PASSES) , MISSISSIPPI RIVER, APRIL 12, 1862

Sir: The court of enquiry assembled to enquire into your conduct on the 10th of April has concluded its investigation, and the record has been forwarded to the Department; and as the court has failed to show cause for your conduct on that occasion, but rather left the inference that it proceeded from a "misconception of my letter, and a desire to serve your country by gaining information of the rebel batteries, etc.", all of which was most unjustifiable under a flag of truce, one of the most sacred of all institutions, as its object is purely one of humanity, and therefore respected by all the nations of the earth, even the most remote and barbarous, it is even difficult to conceive how one so long in the service and of your intelligence could think he had a right to avail himself of such an occasion as the visit of the French captain to violate the usages of war, and at the same time offer an indignity to the officer of a friendly power whom you were ordered to pass up the river by your commander in chief, the circumstances of which were fully explained to you by Lieutenant Commanding Nichols. But as there is a possibility of your conduct being the result of a misconception or an error of judgment, I shall await the decision of the Government in your case instead of taking further action, as I should have done if the court had left any other inference.

Very respectfully, your obedient servant,
D.G. Farragut, Flag Officer

(Stewart, Official Records....,Series I, Volume 18, pp. 113,114.

APPENDIX D-1C
(From the narrative of J. Wilkinson, Executive Officer of the Confederate ironclad Louisiana, in reference to visit with DeCamp when the latter was escorting French Captain Cloué up below the forts)

... A few days previous to the action, I had been sent down the river to communicate, under a flag of truce, with one of the ships of the squadron; and in the course of conversation with my old friend Captain DeCamp, the officer in command of a division of the fleet had been informed by him that they could force the obstructions across the river whenever they pleased, and intended doing so when they were ready. The interview took place in his cabin; and although I indignantly repudiated the idea, I could not help feeling how confidently I would stake life and reputation upon the issue if our situations were reversed. I had noticed many familiar faces among the officers and crew as I passed along the deck a few moments before. Every one was at his station; the guns cast loose for action; and it was in the nature of things, that I should contrast this gallant man of war and all this efficiency and discipline with the iron bound box and crew of "horse marines" which I had just left. But it was in no spirit of depreciation of the gallantry of my comrades, for I was quite sure that they would stand to their guns. The wretched "bowl of Gotham" which had no efficient motive power, and which could not even be got under way, when anchored, without slipping the chain cable, caused the misgivings. It is no disparagement to the prowess of the U. S. fleet which passed the forts, to assert, that they never could have successfully opposed our forces; but the battle was won quite as effectually when they succeeded in passing beyond the range of the guns of the forts and the "Louisiana."
After our official business was closed, DeC.

and I began to talk of the war; and he expressed the opinions then entertained, beyond a doubt, by a majority of U. S. army and naval officers. They believed it to be the intention of the Government to bring the seceding States back into the Union, with their rights and institutions unimpaired. Since then a little leaven has leavened the whole lump, and the former doctrine of the extreme abolitionists has long become the creed of the dominant party. But some facts should be borne in mind by those who denounce slavery as the sum of all villainies; for instance; that the slave code of Massachusetts was the earliest in America; the cruelest in its provisions and has never been formally repealed; that the Plymouth settlers, according to history, maintained "that the white man might own and sell the negro and his offspring forever;" that Mr. Quincy, a representative from Massachusetts during the war of 1812, threatened the House of Congress that the North would secede "peaceably if we can, forcibly if we must" unless their demands for peace were acceded to; and lastly that the abolitionists of a later age denounced the Constitution and canonized John Brown for committing a number of murders and endeavoring to incite servile insurrection in time of peace...

(Wilkinson, J., *The Narrative of a Blockade-Runner*, Sheldon and Company: New York, 1877, pp. 35-37)

APPENDIX D-2A
(Supplemental report of Lieutenant-Colonel Higgins of the Confederacy, Commanding Officer of Forts Jackson and St. Philip, to Lieutenant William M. Bridges, Aid-de-Camp and A.A.A. General, Second Brigade, re: surrender of the forts following mutiny)

NEW ORLEANS, APRIL 30, 1862
Sir: I have the honor to report that on the morning of the 27th April, 1862, a formal demand for a surrender of Forts Jackson and St. Philip was made by Commodore David D. Porter, commanding United States mortar fleet.

The terms which were offered were of the most liberal nature; but so strong was I in the belief that we could resist successfully any attack which could be made upon us, either by land or water, that the terms were at once refused. Our fort was still strong. Our damage had been to some extent repaired. Our men had behaved well, and all was hope and confidence with the officers when suddenly, at midnight, I was aroused by the report that the garrison had revolted, had seized the guard and were spiking the guns. Word was sent us through the sergeants of companies that the men would fight no longer. The company officers were immediately dispatched to their commands, but were driven back. Officers were fired upon when they appeared in sight upon the parapet. Signals were exchanged by the mutineers with Fort St. Philip. The mutiny was complete and a general massacre of the officers and a disgraceful surrender of the fort appeared inevitable.

By great exertion we succeeded, with your influence, in preventing this disgraceful blot upon our country, and were fortunate in keeping the passion of the men in check until we could effect an honorable surrender of the forts, which was done by us, jointly, on the morning of the 28th instant.

As the facts and documents relating to this matter are in your possession, it is unnecessary for me to dwell longer on this humiliating and unhappy affair. I wish to place on record here the noble conduct of Captain Cornay's company, the St. Mary's Cannoneers, who alone stood true as steel when every other company in Fort Jackson basely dishonored their country.

I have the honor to remain,
Very respectfully, your obedient servant,
Ed. Higgins, Lieut. Col., C.S.A.,
Late Commander Forts Jackson and St. Philip

(Stewart, Official Records... ,Series I, Volume 18, pp. 280, 281.)

APPENDIX D-2B
(Extract from report of Confederate Brid. Gen. Duncan to Confederate J. G. Pickett, Asst. Adjt. Gen. , re: mutiny in Ft. Jackson)

... So far, throughout the entire bombardment and final action, the spirit of the troops was cheerful, confident, and courageous. They were mostly foreign enlistments, without any great interests at stake in the ultimate success of the revolution. A reaction set in among them during the lull of the 25th, 26th, and 27th, when there was no other excitement to arouse them than the fatigue duty of repairing our damages and when the rumor was current that the city had surrendered and was then in the hands of the enemy.

No reply had been received from the city to my dispatches sent by couriers on the 24th and 25th, by means of which I could reassure them. They were still obedient, but not buoyant and cheerful. In consequence, I endeavored to revive their courage and patriotism by publishing an order to both garrisons...

I regret to state that it did not produce the desired effect. Everything remained quiet, however, until midnight, when the garrison of Fort Jackson revolted in mass; seized upon the guard and posterns; reversed the fieldpieces commanding the gates, and commenced to spike the guns, while many of the men were leaving the fort in the meantime under arms. All this occurred as suddenly as it was unexpected. The men were mostly drawn up under arms and positively refused to fight any longer, besides endeavoring by force to bring over the St. Mary's Cannoneers and such other few men as remained true to their cause and country.

The mutineers stated that the officers intended to hold out as long as possible, or while the provisions lasted, and then blow up the forts and everything in them; that the city had surrendered, and that there was no further use in fighting: that the enemy were about to attack by land and water on three sides at once, and that a longer defense would only prove a butchery. Every endeavor was made by the officers to repress the revolt and to bring the men to reason and order, but without avail. Officers upon the ramparts were fired upon by the mutineers in attempting to put a stop to the spiking of the guns.

... Being so general among the men, the officers were helpless and powerless to act. Under these circumstances there was but one course left, viz, to let those men go who wished to leave the fort, in order to see the number left and to ascertain what reliance could be placed upon them. About one-half of the garrison left immediately, including men from every company excepting the St. Mary's Cannoneers, volunteers and regulars, non-commissioned officers and privates, and among them many of the very men who had stood last and best to their guns throughout the protracted bombardment and the final action when the enemy passed. It was soon evident that there was no further fight in the men remaining behind...

(Stewart, Official Records...,Series I, Volume 18, pp. 272, 273.)

APPENDIX D-2C

(Letter from President of the United States Abraham Lincoln to Congress, recommending a vote of thanks for Flag-Officer Farragut for his successful campaign at New Orleans)

WASHINGTON, D. C., MAY 14, 1862

The third section of the "Act further to promote the efficiency of the Navy," approved the 21st December, 1861, provides --

That the President of the United States, by and with the advice and consent of the Senate, shall have the authority to detail from the retired list of the Navy, for the command of squadrons and single ships, such officers as he may believe that the good of the service requires to be thus placed in command; and such officers may, if upon the recommendation of the President of the United States they shall receive a vote of thanks of Congress for their services and gallantry in action against an enemy, be restored to the active list, and not otherwise.

In conformity with this law, Captain David G. Farragut was nominated to the Senate for continuance as the flag-officer in command of the squadron which recently rendered such important service to the Union by his successful operation on the lower Mississippi and capture of New Orleans.

Believing that no occasion could arise which more fully correspond with the intention of the law, or be more pregnant with happy influence as an example, I cordially recommend that Captain D.G. Farragut receive a vote of thanks of Congress for his services and gallantry displayed in the capture, since the 21st December, 1861, of Forts Jackson and St. Philip, city of New Orleans, and the destruction of various rebel gunboats, rams, etc.

Abraham Lincoln

To the Senate and House of Representatives

(Stewart, Official Records...,Series I, Volume 18, p. 246.)

APPENDIX D-3A

(Report of Commander Palmer, U.S. Navy, of the U.S.S. Iroquois, to Farragut, regarding the surrender of Baton Rouge.)

**U.S.S. IROQUOIS
AT ANCHOR OFF BATON ROUGE,
MAY 9, 1862**

Sir: Agreeably to your instructions I proceeded up the river and anchored on the evening of the 7th close in abreast this city. I sent an officer on shore to summon the mayor on board, but as he was not in town the next in authority accompanied my officer on his return, and I was informed that the Brooklyn and gunboats had passed up without communicating, and that the mayor and council would, in the morning, be prepared to receive any communication that I might make. I accordingly addressed the enclosed letter, numbered 1, and received in reply that marked No. 2.

Here is a capital of a State with 7,000 inhabitants, acknowledging itself defenseless, and yet assuming an arrogant tone, trusting to our forbearance.

I was determined to submit to no such nonsense, and accordingly weighed anchor and steamed up abreast the arsenal, landed a force, took possession of the arsenal, barracks, and other public property of the United States, and hoisted over it our flag. No resistance was offered.

I then addressed the mayor the communication marked 3, to which No. 4 is the reply, and shortly afterwards the Brooklyn hove in sight, coming down the river and anchoring near us. I reported what I had done to Captain Craven, who thoroughly endorsed my action.

Very respectfully, your obedient servant,
Jas. S. Palmer, Commander

(Stewart, Official Records...,Series I, Volume 18, p. 473.)

APPENDIX D-3B

(Second letter from Mayor of Baton Rouge to Commander Palmer of the U.S.S. Iroquois, regarding the surrender of Baton Rouge.)

MAYOR'S OFFICE
CITY OF BATON ROUGE, MAY 9, 1862

Sir: Your note of this date is received, and I agree with you that war is a sad calamity, and it is greatly to be hoped its horrors will not be visited by the intelligent and Christian commander of a hostile fleet upon the innocent, peaceable, and unoffending citizens within the jurisdiction of the town.

In my former note I disclaimed any jurisdiction over the grounds upon which the arsenal is situated, and to preserve order within the limits of this city has always been and will continue to be my duty.

What depredations may be committed without the limits of Baton Rouge, the authorities of this city can not in fairness be held responsible, and I can not conceive why you should make such requirement of the inhabitants.

A moment's reflection must convince you that you have not, in conscience, morals, or by any rules of international or statutory law, any such right. But should you adhere and hold this city responsible for the acts of men over whom I have no jurisdiction, I ask that before letting loose your dogs of war, you give the women and children and peaceable citizens an opportunity of avoiding the sad calamity.

If there has been to-day any manifestation to interrupt your proceedings at the barracks, you may be assured that none of the citizens of this city were engaged, and neither will they be.

Yours, respectfully,
B. F. Bryan, Mayor

(Stewart, Official Records...,Series I, Volume 18, p. 475.)

APPENDIX D-3C

(Letter from Farragut to B. F. Bryan, Mayor of Baton Rouge, regarding surrender of the city.)

U.S. FLAGSHIP HARTFORD
AT ANCHOR OFF BATON ROUGE,
MAY 10, 1862

Sir: On my arrival before your city, Captain Palmer laid before me his correspondence with your honor for the surrender of the city, and has thus far acted in accordance with my views.

I have no wish to interfere with your municipal authority, but desire that you will continue to exercise your functions as mayor and maintain order in the city, and, as the sole representative of any supposed authority, you will suppress every ensign and symbol of government, whether State or Confederate, except that of the United States, whose flag has already been hoisted, by order of Captain Palmer, on the arsenal, and which I expect will be respected by yourself and others, so far as not to permit it to be disturbed.

I understand that you have a foreign corps employed as a police guard for the maintenance of good order. They will be respected as such and not interfered with, unless General Butler should deem it necessary to take charge of the city, in which case he, or his commandant, will issue his own instructions.

Permit me herewith to forward you a few of his proclamations.

I am, with great respect, your obedient servant,
D.G. Farragut,
Flag-Officer Western Gulf Blockading Squadron

(Stewart, Official Records...,Series I, Volume 18, p. 476.)

APPENDIX D-4A
(Report of Commander Palmer, U.S. Navy, to Farragut, regarding surrender of Natchez)

AT ANCHOR OFF NATCHEZ, MAY 13, 1862
Sir: In obedience to your order of the 10th instant, I left Baton Rouge at 4 in the afternoon of that day and proceeded up the river until I overtook the Oneida and the gunboats, some 40 miles below this, who accompanied me on to my present position off this city, which I reached at 2 on the afternoon of yesterday.

I addressed to the mayor the accompanying letter, marked 1, which they refused to receive at the landing, and the tone seemed to be that of resolute nonintercourse. This conduct being rather more dignified than wise, I instantly seized the ferryboat, then on this side occupied in filling herself with coal, which I intended to secure also, and placing on board of her a force from this squadron, of seamen and marines, and a couple of howitzers, under the command of Lieutenant Harmony, of this ship, sent her across to the landing with orders that, if there were not there some of the authorities to receive my communication, he was to land his force, march up to the town, which was about half a mile distant, with colors flying, and there cause the mayor to receive and read my letter. But when the party had reached the landing they found two members of the common council, sent with an apology from the mayor to receive my communication. They begged that the force should not be landed, as they intended to make no resistance, and seemed disposed to acquiesce in anything I demanded.

The party then returned, and the following morning I received the enclosed reply, numbered 2, together with the proclamation which I also enclose.

The city being now virtually surrendered, and by the proclamation of the mayor so announced to its inhabitants, I concluded to send an officer on shore, to which purpose I sent the note marked No. 3.

In an hour or two, being notified by signal that the committee with an escort was in waiting to receive my officer, I dispatched Lieutenant McNair, of this ship, to ascertain from the mayor whether there were any public buildings from which the rebel flag had been hitherto displayed; if so, it was my intention to hoist there the flag of the United States, which I should require to be guarded and respected by the authorities, also to say that I was as anxious as he was to preserve the peace and quiet of the town: that we were not here to make war upon its peaceful inhabitants, and that I should land no force unless I considered it absolutely necessary. This officer was received most courteously and even kindly by the authorities; the mayor assured him that their flag had never been officially displayed in Natchez: that their Government had no buildings or property in the town, but that if I chose to hoist the flag of the United States the authorities would do their best to protect it, but hoped they would be spared the responsibility for the possible act of an excited populace.

As this city, unlike Baton Rouge, had never occupied a military position, but was simply a trading town, and as its mayor and authorities had behaved in so sensible and gentleman-like a manner, I concluded to leave the question of hoisting the flag open until your arrival, and so informed them.

The policy of my forbearance I submit to your better judgment.

I am very respectfully, your
obedient servant,
Jas. S. Palmer, Commander

(Stewart, Official Records...,Series I, Volume 18, p. 490.)

APPENDIX D-4B

(Letter from John Hunter, Mayor of Natchez, to Jas. S. Palmer, Commander U.S.S. Iroquois anchored off Natchez, re: surrender of Natchez to the Union.)

MAYOR'S OFFICE
NATCHEZ, MISS., MAY 13, 1862

Sir: Your communication of the 12th instant has been received by me and laid before the board of selectmen of this city, and I am directed to return the following reply:

Coming as a conqueror, you need not the interposition of the city authorities to possess this place. An unfortified city, and entirely defenseless people, have no alternative but to yield to an irresistible force, or uselessly to imperil innocent blood. Formalities are absurd in the face of such realities. So far as the city authorities can prevent, there will be no opposition to your possession of the city; they can not, however, guarantee that your flag shall wave unmolested in the sight of an excited people, but such authority as they possess will be exercised for the preservation of good order in the city.

As to property belonging to the Confederate States, they are not aware of any such within the limits of the city.

Very respectfully, your obedient servant,
John Hunter, Mayor

(Stewart, Official Records...,Series I, Volume 18, pp. 490, 491.)

APPENDIX D-5A

(Letter from Commander Porter to Captain Craven about Lt. Woodworth's allegations re: contrabands removed from his protection)

U.S.S. OCTORARA
MISSISSIPPI RIVER, JUNE 24, 1862

Sir: A midshipman from the Iroquois has come with a verbal order to take any contrabands he may find on the Mortar Flotilla or anywhere else. There are a number who have come on board in the river, and while here, and they have been provided for according to law, waiting for the flag-officer's decision in regard to them. The regulation of the Navy Department, of which the enclosed is a copy, issued by Flag-Officer Goldsborough, requires that contrabands claiming protection shall be enlisted at $8, $9, and $10 per month, according to circumstances, and when vacancies have occurred in the flotilla, they have been filled by those we have picked up on the river, of able-bodied men. I should be very glad to get rid of some of those on board, could I do so without violating the law, which enacts that contrabands belonging to rebels shall not be given up by officers of the Army or Navy.

Will you please to give me a written order to this effect? I would not, of my own accord, give up these people (who come to us for protection) to a brutal overseer, or to parties who claim to be Union now, though at the same time the difficulties of keeping them are very great and there is no knowing how many may come hereafter. I sent them away at first to other vessels, or passed them on the river, but they come on board now at night, and I can not, according to my understanding of the law and wishes of the Government, refuse to receive them. A written order from you will settle the matter at once, and I can not take the verbal order of a midshipman in a case of this kind without knowing explicitly what it is that you desire to be done in the premises.

Very respectfully, your obedient servant,
David D. Porter
Commanding Mortar Fleet

(Stewart, Official Records...,Series I, Volume 18, pp. 571, 572.)

APPENDIX D-5B
(Report of Acting Lieutenant Woodworth of the U.S.S. John P. Jackson, to Commander D.D. Porter of the Mortar Flotilla, regarding contrabands, or slaves)

U.S.S. JOHN P. JACKSON
OFF VICKSBURG, JULY 1, 1862
Sir: It becomes my duty to report to you that in carrying out my instructions, in compliance with the act of Congress and instructions from the Navy Department in relation to contrabands, I was compelled to receive all those seeking refuge on board the U.S.S. Jackson, my vessel being stationed at the head of the line of the fleet, and first meeting those coming down the river.

Up to the morning of the 24th of June I had enlisted and given shelter to 47 persons, including men, women, and children, who had sought protection of my vessel under a flag of truce.

The enclosed list includes only those taken from the island, and from intelligence I received from those already in my custody, and from efforts made by some I had permitted to return, that accessions would soon be made to the number of 2,000 for the purpose of constructing the "cut-off," I deemed it expedient to establish a camp on an island in the river, near the anchorage of the squadron.

Twenty of the men on the island were regularly enlisted from time to time under the law governing such cases, and were employed as coal passers and other various duties on board, and to whom clothing and rations had been regularly issued. They were at this time engaged on the island cutting wood for this vessel, the Jackson at the time being without coal and no supply vessel in the squadron.

An officer came on board my vessel and informed me that he came by order of Commander Craven, of the Brooklyn, to demand all contrabands in my custody and all others that may be found on board of any vessel belonging to the Mortar Flotilla.

I informed him that I had a large number of contrabands in my custody, consisting of men, women, and children, but that not having accommodations on board the steamer, I had placed them in camp on the island, where my men were employed cutting wood for the Jackson, by your order.

I directed the officer to return to Commander Craven and inform him that I would immediately confer with Commander Porter in person, and ordered him not to remove or molest any person on the island until I received Commander Porter's instructions what to do. I assured the officer that the contrabands would be safe in my charge until Commander Porter could communicate with Commander Craven.

I also directed the officer to inform Commander Craven that 20 of the men were regularly enlisted on board my vessel, and to whom issues of clothing and rations had been made, and that I would require a written order for their transfer and receipts for their accounts.

I proceeded immediately to inform you of the demand of Commander Craven, and while on board the Octorara the officer or officers sent by Commander Craven removed from the island all the contrabands I had placed there. On returning to my vessel I learned that the island, containing much public property, was left without protection.

The 40 contrabands taken from the island belonged to, or were claimed by, persons residing on plantations for 300 miles distant. The whole were taken, as alleged, to be returned to their owner, a woman residing opposite Vicksburg, who had been on board the Iroquois and Brooklyn and represented herself as a loyal subject to the Union: but I have reasons to know, from reports from her own negroes and from information obtained by my officers, that she is the wife of a notorious rebel. Both husband and wife have ever and continue to afford aid and comfort to the enemy, and since the return of her negroes has had concealed in her house a rebel spy for several days, who would have been captured by a party from my ship but for the assistance of the woman who aided his escape.

The barbarous and inhuman treatment received by these unoffending slaves at the hands and under the direction of this woman since their restoration, can only be understood by seeing them since their scourging.

I am pained to think that I should have been the innocent cause of this brutal chastisement that took place almost within sight and sound of our squadron, when I had promised them immunity from punishment, as I believed I had authority to do under the instructions contained in the circular of the Secretary of the Navy concerning contrabands.

Many of those who were returned to their owners by Commander Craven assured me they were induced to leave their masters by reports among them that they would never again be returned after once reaching the aegis of our flag and guns.

Under the peculiar circumstances that I am situated, having no paymaster on board and being held responsible pecuniarily for issues of public property under my charge, I have to request that I may be instructed how to proceed in order to protect myself from the responsibility I have assumed under your verbal orders, and at the same time to be governed in future, to prevent a recurrence of the very humiliating position I have been placed in by this unwarranted and unofficial act of Commander Craven.

I have the honor to be, very respectfully, your obedient servant,

Selim E. Woodworth,
Acting Lieutenant, Commanding

Stewart, Official Records...,Series I, Volume 18, pp. 665-666.

APPENDIX D-6
(Letter from Farragut to Major-General Butler of the Army, re: officers' opinion about attacking Vicksburg)

U.S. GUNBOAT KENNEBEC
BELOW VICKSBURG, MAY 22, 1862
Dear General: I received your kind note, together with the mail, by the steamer Fox. My ship had got off and was about 40 or 50 miles below Vicksburg, at Grand Gulf, which is the most dangerous part of the river, and beyond which I am unwilling to risk the large ships.

It appears to be the general opinion here among the officers, General Williams included, that there is very little use in attacking Vicksburg, as the guns on the heights are so elevated that our fire will not be felt by them. As they have so large a force of soldiers here, several thousand in and about the town, and the facility of bringing in 20,000 in an hour by railroad from Jackson, altogether (I) think it would be useless to bombard it, as we could not hold it if we take it. Therefore we have determined to blockade it and occasionally harass them with fire until the battle of Corinth shall decide its fate. General Williams is going up the Red River, where he thinks he may be more useful, and I have given him a gunboat to accompany him. I shall soon drop down the river again, as I consider my services indispensably necessary on the seaboard. I am greatly obliged to you for your kindness in towing up my coal vessels. I do not see that I can be of any service here, and I do not see as General Williams will be of any use here with the small force he has. I shall endeavor to get down as soon as possible.

Very respectfully, your obedient servant,
D.G. Farragut

I have already supplied your troops with as much bread as I could spare, as well as pork. They have been able thus far, I think, to get fresh beef, but are much in want of bread and flour.

(Stewart, *Official Records...,Series I, Volume 18, p. 507*)

APPENDIX D-7
(*Letter from Farragut to Lt. Russell of the Kennebec, re: frustration and disappointment that Kennebec did not pass Vicksburg, instead remaining downriver*)

U.S. FLAGSHIP HARTFORD
ABOVE VICKSBURG, JULY 5, 1862
Sir: Your report of your attack on Vicksburg, etc., has been duly received, and I regret to observe that you also quote my general order as a justification for not coming up the river, which I can not recognize as a valid reason: although I stated that the ships were to drop down again in my general order, it was naturally to be inferred that I was to be the judge when it was to be done, and I think you must remember that I distinctly stated to you and the other commanding officers that the old signal was to be made of tack, or wear, beginning at the rear, but the general order certainly stated that you were to go up to the bend of the river before dropping down again. I can not, therefore, comprehend why you did not pass above the mortar boats without waiting for them to drop down below you. Had you simply stated that you followed the Brooklyn and remained with her, I could have recognized the reasoning, but I can not justify your interpretation of my general order.

Your report of the loss of an anchor and cable down the river has also been received.

Very respectfully, your obedient servant,
D.G. Farragut

(*Stewart, Official Records...,Series I, Volume 18, p. 602.*)

APPENDIX D-8
(*Report of Lieutenant Lowry to Captain Craven of the U.S.S. Brooklyn about conversation with owner of large plantation who was resistant to Confederate government*)

U.S. STEAM SLOOP BROOKLYN
OFF BELLE VIEW PLANTATION, LA.,
MISSISSIPPI RIVER, APRIL 12, 1862
Sir: In obedience to your order, I proceeded on shore to the plantations near this anchorage for the purpose of communicating with the owners or residents, and of obtaining some fresh provisions for the officers and crew. On arriving at the levee I was met by a large crowd of negroes, of all ages and sexes, who seemed happy and contented. On making enquiry, I ascertained that the plantation, with

five neighboring ones, belonged to a Colonel J. Acklin (Ackland?) [Lowry's parentheses], who was on his resident plantation, some 3 miles distant. I dispatched a messenger for him and in a short time he came up on horseback, met me very cordially, indeed warmly, expressing great pleasure in seeing us. He was laboring under intense excitement caused by having just received an imperative order from a captain of an irregular band of militia to burn his cotton within five days or to run the risk of having it burned for him, with the additional threat of hanging him for noncompliance. I stated to him my mission, which was to procure fresh beef and vegetables, for which we would pay a fair market price, and at the same time assured him that private property, life, and honor were safe under the protection of the United States naval forces, as long as not held by persons in armed rebellion against the Federal Government. He replied to the former that he had no provisions: that he had over 1,000 negroes to feed and clothe: that such was the scarcity of all kinds of food that his people greatly suffered: that they had had no meat of any kind for three weeks: that his negroes had liberty to raise their own poultry, vegetables, etc., which they had his free permission to sell to us. In reply to the latter, he gave me a history of his persecutions and sacrifices in and for the so-called Confederate States Government. He stated that the men of substance had been constantly pressed by that Government and its troops for money, provisions, teams, wagons, and negroes, and that he had been ordered to burn his cotton time after time, which he had steadily and resolutely refused to do. He represented to me that he raised from 5,000 to 6,000 bales of cotton a year; that he had all of last year's crop unsold, and for the sale of it he depended for supplying his slaves with food and raiment, and that every principle of right, law, and justice forbid him to burn it. That though he was a Southern man, with large Southern interests, perhaps the wealthiest man in Louisiana, he had every confidence that the North was actuated according to their own ideas with the principle of justice and civilization, and were, in a word, gentlemen. That he had taken no active part in the rebellion, but had been on his plantation the whole year—separated from his family who resided in Nashville—taking care of his property and slaves. Much that this gentleman said will go to show the loyal men of the North under what a system of tyranny our unhappy countrymen of the South have been brought to by the wicked acts of the few demagogues who have inaugurated and led this most unnatural revolt. Colonel Acklin said that the people had been driven into this war by misrepresentations of the acts and intentions of the North against the South. That men who had nothing to lose were intent on lowering to their own positions all who had. He represented that in the Red River country Davis would never get another man or dollar for the war. That if things went on as they were now going, a reaction would soon take place, which would end in fearful bloodshed, and that the leaders who had misled and ruined them would yet meet with public vengeance. He denounced in no measured terms Governors Moore, of Louisiana, and Pettus, of Mississippi, as having had a most baneful influence upon the people in their States. I have given the sum of this gentleman's remarks in brief, and altogether his description of transactions during the year, with the notice just served on him to wantonly destroy his property, made up a picture of misery, political degradations, and military despotism almost incredible. Incredible that men born under a free government, with the right of speech and suffrage, should in so short a time be brought under the iron heel of a remorseless and cruel tyranny. The suffering of this planter, I was led to understand, was not an isolated case. Nearly all the cotton which had been destroyed on this river since our occupation, on the grounds of preventing its falling into our hands, has been so destroyed under coercive threats, with promises from those in power to remunerate the owners by the Confederate Government at the end of the war and the recognition of the independence of the South. I received information that large bodies of men, though badly fed, clothed, armed and disciplined, had been crossing the river near this place from the Red River country. These men were making their way to Corinth, but since the appearance of our naval forces all travel had been stopped, and troops had ceased to cross. A large number of river steamers were up the Red River. It was represented to me that it was absolutely necessary, to preserve the lives of the inhabitants of the plantations on the river banks, that supplies of beef, bread, flour, bacon, etc., should arrive speedily, and I was implored to represent that the opening of the commerce, or river trade, would be hailed with joy and satisfaction. I was led to understand that numerous guerrilla bands were forming in the hill country back of the river. These bands were marauding and levying upon the planters. Should our army prove victorious at Corinth, and the rebel army be destroyed or dispersed, great numbers of lawless soldiers will no doubt swell these bands and for a long time keep the country in a distracted state. A rigid administration of martial law to a few ringleaders would have a wholesome effect. In conclusion, with an apology for expressing my sentiments, in what should perhaps be strictly an official report, I beg leave to say that I gathered sufficient information to convince me that little resistance will be made to the laws of the United States and the Constitution by the people of wealth and weight in the Southern community. A false notion of what their honor and dignity might exact would perhaps prompt them to hold out in the maintenance of their principles, but that the return to peace, plenty, and security in life and property of all kinds that the power and virtue of our beloved Government would secure, will be hailed with secret joy by all who have anything to lose by the privation of those elements of human happiness, I have not the slightest doubt. The offer of armed protection to Colonel Acklin was courteously declined on the ground that it would subject him to the fury of the mob after the force was withdrawn; but he assured me that he would protect his property against the "Davis emissaries" with his life. After offering a number of late Northern newspapers, with General Butler's proclamation, which were politely and gratefully received, our interview ended, and I left this gentleman with the melancholy reflection that his vast estates and great wealth were no protection to him in a region where all government had ended, and only the unbridled passions of men ruled the hour, and more convinced of the necessity of the United States Government extending its protecting arms over its offending yet deluded and helpless children, to save them from utter ruin and degradation.

I am, very respectfully, your obedient servant,
R. B. Lowry,
Lieutenant, U.S.Navy

(Stewart, Charles, Official Records..., Series I, Volume 18, pp. 125 - 127)

APPENDIX D-9

(Report from Farragut to Secretary of the Navy Gideon Welles, about scurvy among ships of fleet)

FLAGSHIP HARTFORD
NEW ORLEANS, JULY 29, 1862

Sir: On my arrival at Ship Island, if the Santee has not already gone north, I will send her home immediately, as I hear that the scurvy is raging to a frightful degree on board of her. We have had as high as 80 on the sick list, and in some of the ships 100, but the cases have, with but few exceptions, proved mild: they recover slowly, and I am in hopes that the sea air will bring them up.

I would like to let the men go on liberty here: they are so anxious for it, and feel the confinement on shipboard so much that it makes them dissatisfied. I will do so if I can and where I can, as I think satisfaction is a great element in war.

Very respectfully, your obedient servant,
D.G. Farragut

(Stewart, Official Records...,Series I, Volume 19, p. 98.)

APPENDIX D-10

(Report from Commodore Thatcher to Secretary of the Navy Gideon Welles about the U.S.S. Kanawha's capture of the schooner Albert, or Wenona)

U.S. STEAM FRIGATE COLORADO
OFF MOBILE BAY, NOVEMBER 30, 1863

Sir: I have the honor to report the capture of the schooner, Albert, or Wenona, William Henry Belden, master, by the gunboat Kanawha, Lieutenant-Commander W.K. Mayo.

This schooner had been loaded many weeks, awaiting an opportunity of escaping from Mobile, and last night she made the attempt to run out, but was captured soon after passing the bar, and is now under orders for New Orleans in charge of Acting Master Levi S. Fickett, with all the papers and documents required by law, to be delivered to the U.S. district judge at that place.

Lists of the officers and crews of the vessels serving on this blockade at the time of the capture will be forwarded as soon as received the several commanding officers.

The Albert had neither log book, crew list, nor custom-house papers. The supposed owner, Boyd, was a passenger on board: also a young man as passenger, and her crew is composed of seven men.

Her cargo is valuable, and consists of 245 bales of cotton, 100 barrels rosin, 15 barrels turpentine, 13 boxes tobacco, 20 caddies tobacco, and 1,000 staves. On the persons of passengers and crew were found papers of value, also money and implements. The aggregate of current money found will be $5,572, mostly in specie, besides a large amount in railroad bonds. This money and bonds are in the keeping of Acting Assistant Paymaster L.L. Penniman, of the Kanawha, a receipt for which is herein enclosed.

I have the honor to be, very respectfully, your obedient servant,
H.H. Thatcher
Commodore

(Stewart, Official Records...,Series I, Volume 21, p. 704.)

APPENDIX D-11

(Two reports of Commodore Thatcher to Commodore Bell about the capture of the rebel schooner John Scott)

**U.S. STEAM FRIGATE COLORADO,
OFF MOBILE BAY, JANUARY 8, 1864**

Sir: Herewith I forward the report of Lieutenant-Commander William P. McCann, commanding U.S. gunboat Kennebec, of the capture of Confederate schooner John Scott, from Mobile for Havana, with cargo of cotton and turpentine:

At 1:30 a.m., while at anchor in main ship channel, I discovered a small boat drifting out to sea. The cable was slipped and the boat picked up with a Mobile pilot named William Norval, from whom I learned that he had piloted out the Swash Channel the evening previous the rebel blockade runner John Scott. I immediately steamed to the southward and eastward and about 8 a.m. discovered a sail to the southward and gave chase and fired a shot to heave her to. She did not hoist her colors, but commenced throwing overboard part of her deck load of cotton and hauled by the wind to the southward and westward. On coming within range I opened fire, and at the tenth shot she rounded to and was boarded and proved to be the rebel schooner John Scott, bound from Mobile to Havana with cotton and turpentine, and the same vessel the pilot Scott (Norval) had brought out of Mobile Bay the evening previous. The papers found on board proved her to be a rebel. I at once transferred the master and five other persons to this vessel as prisoners, took her in tow, and returned to this squadron. I have transmitted all the papers and writings found on board to the U.S. district judge at the port of New Orleans. This vessel is an American-built pilot boat, built at Newburgh, N.Y., and her foreign name was Victoria. The only colors found on board were an English and a Confederate flag. There was no other vessel in sight at the time of the capture...

The following is a list of persons found on board the J. Scott, viz: William Brown, captain, Liverpool; John Mahoney, sailor, England; Charles Johnson, sailor, Sweden; N.A. Bowford, sailor, Nassau, New Providence; Alexander Sabio, Italy; S.D. Handcock, cook, Liverpool.

Very respectfully, your obedient servant,
H.K. Thatcher,
Commodore

(Second letter from Thatcher to Bell regarding the John Scott)

**U.S. STEAM FRIGATE COLORADO
OFF MOBILE BAY, JANUARY 8, 1864**

Commodore: I deem the information communicated to me by Lieutenant-Commander McCann of sufficient importance to make it the subject of an especial letter. This William Norval, the pilot who brought out the prize schooner John Scott, now a prisoner, is sent to New Orleans to be delivered to your orders with the crew of the prize. He is the man who piloted out all the blockade runners, according to his own confession, and therefore a very important personage to the rebels, and had he been able to return to Mobile would doubtless have been employed by that Government to pilot their armed vessels should they conclude to make a raid upon this squadron, and you will perceive the importance of retaining this prisoner in security. From all accounts Mobile pilots are now very much reduced in numbers and difficult to be procured.

I am, sir, very respectfully, your obedient servant,
H.K. Thatcher,
Commodore

(Stewart, Official Records...,Series I, Volume 21, pp. 15, 16.)

APPENDIX D-12
(Farragut's report regarding difficulties of taking Fort Powell at Grant's Pass)

U.S. FLAGSHIP HARTFORD
OFF SHIP ISLAND, FEBRUARY 28, 1864

Sir: I have been shelling Fort Powell, on Shell Island, in Grant's Pass, Mississippi Sound, during the past week, but have made but little impression upon it, as we can not approach nearer than 4,000 yards, and then we got hard aground in the Calhoun, drawing only 8 1/2 feet. It required two steamers besides her own power to get her off. This I did because I saw the wind hauling round to the northward, which blows the water out of the sound, and I feared we might be kept there a week or longer before the water would rise sufficiently to enable us to get off. The enemy at the time were throwing their shot three-fourths of a mile over and beyond us. The ammunition of the vessels being nearly all expended, and fearing I might not receive a supply in less than two days, I hauled all the vessels out where they could float.

The weather became thick and has continued so for the last two days. I have now received a fresh supply of ammunition and will recommence the work tomorrow, the 29th, but I have no hope of reducing the fort, as the steamers lie on the opposite side of it to take the people aboard, if necessary, or to relieve the garrison.

We cannot get within 800 yards in the small boats, so as to assault it, but it assists General Sherman by keeping up the idea of an attack upon Mobile, which is looked for hourly by the Confederates. Would that were true; now is the propitious time.

The Tennessee is at Mobile getting the camels under her, and if their intention is to get her over Dog River Bar, which I doubt, she will have to take the chances of being destroyed in doing so.

If we had only two or three thousand troops to make their approaches on the peninsulas the ships will run in, I think, easily. We might have done it long since, but General Banks is ordered to be ready to move in concert with General Sherman, and of course is not willing to risk being out of place at the moment he is called upon to march.

After the Tennessee gets over Dog River Bar it would be imprudent to go in without an ironclad, as I before stated, because she could lie in shoal water where our ships could not get at her, and could knock our vessels to pieces, but if we go in before she gets over the bar, our gunboats will destroy her on the bar if she attempts to cross with camels.

I am ready the moment the army will act with me, but there is no doing anything with forts so long as their back doors are open; besides which my communication must be open for supplies, which can not be done without troops to cut off all their forts from the land communication with Mobile.

Very respectfully, your obedient servant,
D.G. Farragut,
Rear-Admiral, Comdg. Western Gulf Blockdg. Squadron.

(Stewart, Official Records..., Series I, Volume 21, pp. 96, 97.)

BIBLIOGRAPHY

Anonymous. *Dictionary of American Fighting Ships, Volume III.* Washington: Navy Department, Office of the Chief of Naval Operations, Naval History Division, 1968.

Catton, Bruce. *The Civil War.* New York: Fairfax Press, 1980.

Foote, Shelby. *The Civil War: A Narrative.* New York: Random House, 1963.

Frothingham, Jessie Peabody. *Sea Fighters from Drake to Farragut.* New York: Charles Scribner's Sons, 1905.

Headley, Hon. J.T. *Farragut and Our Naval Commanders.* New York: E.B. Treat and Co., Publishers, 1867.

Headley, J.T. *The Great Rebellion, vol. 1.* Hartford, Conn: The American Publishing Co., 1866.

Hoehling, A.A. *Damn the Torpedoes!* Winston-Salem, North Carolina: John F. Blair, Publisher, 1989.

Lewis, Charles Lee. *David Glasgow Farragut, Our First Admiral.* Annapolis: United States Naval Institute, 1943.

Mahan, A.T. *The Gulf and Inland Waters.* New York: Charles Scribner's Sons, 1888.

Miller, Francis Trevelyan, editor-in-chief. *Photographic History of the Civil War.* New York: Review of Reviews, 1911.

Pratt, Fletcher. *Civil War in Pictures.* New York: Henry Holt and Company, 1955.

Stewart, Charles. *Official Records of the Union and Confederate Navies in the War of the Rebellion, Series I - Volumes 18, 19, 20 and 21, West Gulf Blockading Squadron.* Washington: Government Printing Office, 1904.